CONSPIRACY THEORIES

CONTENTS

CONSPIRACY THEORIES

igloobooks

igloobooks

This edition published in 2013
by Igloo Books Ltd
Cottage Farm
Sywell
NN6 0BJ
www.igloobooks.com

Copyright © 2013 Igloo Books Ltd

SHE001 0913
2 4 6 8 10 9 7 5 3 1
ISBN: 978-1-78197-926-6

Written by Will Bryan

Printed and manufactured in China

Москва-Кремль - Moscou-Kremlin   Общій Видъ - Vue générale.

The Barnum & Bailey Greatest Show on Earth

FIRST APPEARANCE IN AMERICA OF THE FAMOUS CONTINENTAL FAVORITES

THE FLYING DILLONS

IN A SERIES OF MOST MARVELOUS MID-AIR FEATS AND STARTLING PERFORM...

THE WORLD'S GRANDEST, LARGEST BEST A...

Above: Tales of unknown species, human or other, continue to intrigue us. This creature is Shwe-Maong, or "hairy man," from Burma, illustrated in a French magazine of 1842.

AT A GLANCE

Conspiracies and hoaxes fall into often distinct categories. Scientific (the Apollo Moon landing was faked); political (Kennedy was the victim of a plot not a lone gunman); world government/big business (the Iraq War was to send oil to China, a secret World Government runs everything); religious (Freemasons run the world); and popular (Elvis Presley is still alive). Hoaxes, such as crop circles and the Cardiff Giant, add light and color to darker conspiratorial tones.

HISTORY'S MYSTERIES

Often history is written or told by people who want to keep some things hidden, and truth is the casualty. Conspiracy theorists, aware that not all the information has been revealed, tend to see secret plots behind the world's great events. They see the world in terms of megalomaniac secret societies, controlling regimes, criminal gangs, terrorists and aliens.

Hoaxes, likewise, play on the idea of half-truths and deception, and are deliberate attempts to make mischief either just for the fun of it or for financial gain. Piltdown Man, for example, was not prehistoric, Barnum's Feejee mermaid never swam in the sea, and the Cottingley fairies flew out of the pages of a child's picture book. But no real harm was done to anyone.

Plenty of real mysteries still baffle us: what happened to the *Mary Celeste*, who was Jack the Ripper, do the Yeti and Loch Ness Monster really exist? Arguments continue over real-life stories such as the shootings of Robert Kennedy and Martin Luther King, the last days of the Romanovs in Russia, and the Cambridge spies. Mysteries often lurch into unbelievable fictions, such as the idea that UFOs from Venus gave free rides to people in the 1950s, or Jack the Ripper returned in the evening to Buckingham Palace!

History is littered with genuine plots, real villainy and lots of mistakes. Moles burrowing for secrets, sex in high places, unsolved murders, cover-ups and deceptions. Conspiracies can alter history. What if Guy Fawkes *had* blown up Parliament in 1605? What if aliens *did* crash in New Mexico in 1948? And if President Kennedy had not gone to Dallas in 1963…?

In this book the weird and wonderful sit alongside history and hoax. Often the most credible answer is: what happened, happened.

FILE

Above: The *Mary Celeste* was a genuine sea mystery of the 19th century, in an age when stories of ghost ships, sea serpents and mermaids were still credible to many people.

Left: The macabre Jack the Ripper murder mystery of 1888 has enduring appeal, partly because it was never solved.

ASSASSINATIONS

Who killed them, and why? The deaths of well-known people continue to be discussed often long after their lives and achievements have started to fade into history.

Many people who know little of President Abraham Lincoln's politics know that he was shot while watching a play. Many people alive in 1963 remember where they were the day JFK was shot, and many others share in the conspiracy theories about who fired or inspired that fateful shot. The deaths of Robert Kennedy and Martin Luther King, murdered in 1968, also cause comment and controversy to this day. Websites teem with views on how and when the US tried to get rid of Cuba's Fidel Castro, or what went on between Rasputin and the Romanov rulers of Russia before the Communist Revolution of 1917. Fact and fiction become interleaved, whodunnit theories proliferate, and the conspiracy behind the assassin's bullet becomes more impenetrable still, darker than the deed itself.

NOVEMBER 1963

WHO SHOT JFK?

Above: Lee Harvey Oswald tried to kill Major General Edwin A. Walker on April 10, 1963. His garbled writings revealed a man with a grudge against the US political establishment.

Below: On 22 November, 1963, Howard Brennan was standing opposite the Texas School Book Depository in Dallas. From this vantage point, he saw a man at a 6th-floor window (A) shoot with a rifle. Below the shooter, Brennan saw people at a 5th-floor window (B) watching the motorcade pass by.

Who shot President Kennedy? His shooting in Dallas has kept conspiracy theorists busy ever since that fateful day in 1963.

President John F. Kennedy died at 1:00 pm on November 22, 1963, in Parkland Hospital, Dallas. At 12:30 pm the President and Mrs Kennedy had been in a motorcade passing the Texas School Book Depository. Kennedy waved to the crowd. Three shots rang out. The first missed, the second passed through the President's neck and hit Texas Governor John Connally. The third struck Kennedy in the head, fatally. At 1:15 pm, Dallas policeman J. D. Tippit was shot dead trying to stop and question a man. The killer ran into a cinema, where he was arrested. He was Lee Harvey Oswald.

What was the evidence against Oswald? Policeman Marrion Baker saw Oswald leaving the Book Depository building, where a rifle was found. Oswald had rifle training in the US Marines, but some experts doubted he was a crack marksman. Conspiracy theorists question whether Oswald could have fired three shots in under 8 seconds. Oswald had spent time in the Soviet Union, and had a Russian wife. So was he a pro-Communist fanatic, or had he been set up by a bigger conspiracy to get rid of Kennedy? Did Oswald act alone? Or was there a second shooter?

Oswald was charged with double murder (Kennedy and Tippit), but never reached a courtroom. On November 24, while Oswald was being moved to the county jail, nightclub owner Jack Ruby pushed through reporters and shot Oswald, who died soon afterward. This sparked more questions. How had the Dallas police let Ruby get so close with a .38 gun, yelling "You killed the President, you rat!" Was Ruby part of the conspiracy? He died in 1967, from cancer, leaving the mystery unsolved.

NAME

EVIDENCE?

Oswald bought a rifle by mail order, and it's alleged this was the weapon recovered from the School Book Depository. He used a revolver to kill Officer Tippit. Later, it was suggested that Oswald had defected to the Soviet Union and the real assassin was a Russian agent. It was argued that the US government suppressed the fact to avoid a third World War. The body was exhumed in 1981, but was declared to be that of Lee Harvey Oswald.

Left: President and Mrs Kennedy rode through Dallas in a motorcade. In the front seat of the presidential car was Texas state governor John B. Connally, wounded in the shooting.

Below: Poster for Oliver Stone's film about the Kennedy killing, in which Kevin Costner played New Orleans attorney Jim Garrison. Garrison pursued the idea that the killing was the result of a conspiracy.

AUGUST SEPTEMBER OCTOBER **NOVEMBER 1963**

Above: At 11:21 pm Dallas time, Jack Ruby shoots the handcuffed Oswald, having walked into the garage from the Western Union office while the jail entrance was unguarded.

Below: Vice-President Lyndon B. Johnson was sworn in as the 36th President of the United States at 2:39 pm inside Air Force One. Eight minutes later, the plane took off for Washington DC, carrying JFK's body.

Experts pored over the evidence, including cine-film taken by onlooker Abraham Zapruder. There were stories of a second gunman on a grassy knoll, who fled on a motorcycle. A myriad theories and allegations were aired about who wanted Kennedy dead—political rivals, anti-Catholics, Cubans, Russians, the Mafia, union bosses. Websites, books and films still explore the events of that day, many casting doubt on the official verdict. One theory aired in a book and on TV centered on one of the motorcade Secret Service agents, who (it was claimed) shot Kennedy by accident from the following car. A policeman claimed it was this agent's first time in the follow car, with an unfamiliar weapon, which went off either when the car stopped suddenly or in reaction to the first shot. The allegation, supposedly covered up by the government, on the orders of Johnson and Robert Kennedy, was strongly denied and contested by the agent (now dead). All that is clear is that after 1963, public life was never the same for any US political leader.

Left: Mrs Kennedy and the dead president's brother Bobby leave the Capitol after John Kennedy's funeral. Within five years, Bobby too would be assassinated.

Below: The Newmans, spectators at the presidential motorcade, fall to the grass seconds after the shots were fired. Some Secret Service agents thought gunfire came from the grassy knoll behind.

NAME

THE TRUTH?

In 1964, US Chief Justice Earl Warren's Commission concluded that Oswald had acted alone. In 1978 a committee of the House of Representatives accepted evidence that shots came from two locations and that Kennedy "was probably assassinated as a result of a conspiracy". In 1982 the US National Research Council disagreed, but by then the conspiracy "suspects" in the frame included Lyndon Johnson, FBI boss J. Edgar Hoover, the Mafia, Cuban exiles (or Castro), the Soviet KGB, right-wing Republicans and fanatical anti-Catholics.

JANUARY FEBRUARY MARCH **APRIL 1968**

Above: The FBI issued a "Wanted" poster for James Earl Ray. He fled the country, but was caught at London's Heathrow Airport. He pleaded guilty and received a 99-year prison term. In 1977 Ray escaped from jail for three days. He died in prison in 1998, aged 70.

Below: Investigators on the balcony of Room 306 of the Lorraine Motel in Memphis, Tennessee, where Reverend Martin Luther King was shot dead on April 4, 1968.

WHO KILLED KING?

US civil rights activist Martin Luther King was shot dead on April 4, 1968. King had enemies, but many more friends who admired his achievements. So who assassinated this man of peace?

Was King the victim of a conspiracy? Some of those closest to him believed so, and in 1999 a civil trial reaffirmed this view. Jesse Jackson, civil rights leader and a colleague of King, was quoted in 2004 alleging there were "saboteurs" within the civil rights movement. Jackson could not accept that King's killer was escaped convict James Earl Ray. King had been the frequent target of racist attacks, including the bombing of his home. In April 1968, King was in Memphis, Tennessee, to support striking garbage workers. He was shot while standing on his motel balcony. The Civil Rights Act of 1968 marked a major step toward the equality for which he had striven.

CONFIDENTIAL
★ TOP SECRET ★

Above: The Poor People's March in Washington, DC—a campaign begun by King in 1968. His support for such movements, and his opposition to the Vietnam War, are possible reasons that power-brokers wanted him removed.

Left: Famed for his 1963 "I have a dream" speech, Nobel Laureate Martin Luther King was America's most high-profile civil rights leader, and an eloquent spokesman for African-Americans and the underprivileged. This high profile made him a target.

NAME

🗀 AT A GLANCE

King's death provoked grief, rage and riots across America. Public figures often attract the interest—sometimes murderous—of loners and attention-seekers. But was Ray such a man? In 1978, a US Congress committee suggested there was a "likelihood" that Ray did not act alone in killing Dr King. Ray himself, known to have racist views, claimed a man named Raul had been involved, and blamed the US government. Ballistic tests proved inconclusive.

MARCH APRIL MAY **JUNE 1968**

ROBERT KENNEDY KILLED

The world was shocked in 1968 by the killing of Robert (Bobby) Kennedy, brother of the murdered president, John F. Kennedy. Was the killer a lone gunman, as charged, or was Kennedy another conspiracy victim?

Conspiracy theorists dispute the verdict that the killer was Sirhan Sirhan alone, and look for evidence of a conspiracy by people with a grudge against Bobby Kennedy. He had made enemies as a campaigning lawyer investigating links between organized crime and corrupt union bosses, and as a civil rights supporter. In 1960 he helped John Kennedy win the presidential election. He then served as attorney-general, first to President Kennedy and then to President Johnson. Many Americans saw "RFK" as the natural heir to "JFK." In 1968, the Kennedy bandwagon was rolling. Senator Kennedy was well placed to secure the Democratic nomination for president and succeed Lyndon Johnson —and then he was shot. Sirhan claimed to have no memory of his actions, but also said he'd killed Kennedy because Bobby supported Israel. Conspiracy theorists allege a second gunman, possibly a girl in a polka-dot dress seen running away. Controversy focused on the fatal shots. Audio recordings suggested more shots were fired than the eight Sirhan's gun held. Sirhan's "amnesia", it was claimed, was the result of mind-control, maybe by CIA or Mafia controllers.

Above: Bobby Kennedy with civil rights leader Martin Luther King. The deaths of both these leading figures in the same year shocked the people of America.

Above: Kennedy lived with his wife and 11 children at their large family house, Hickory Hill, in Virginia.

Left: The Ambassador Hotel, Los Angeles, where Kennedy was killed. Famed for the Coconut Grove nightclub, the hotel was demolished in 2005.

FILE

Below: Bobby Kennedy lies stricken on the floor of the Ambassador Hotel in Los Angeles after being shot at close range.

Right: A 1967 reel-to-reel tape recorder. Audiotape recordings analyzed in 2007 suggested possibly as many as 11 shots were fired in total.

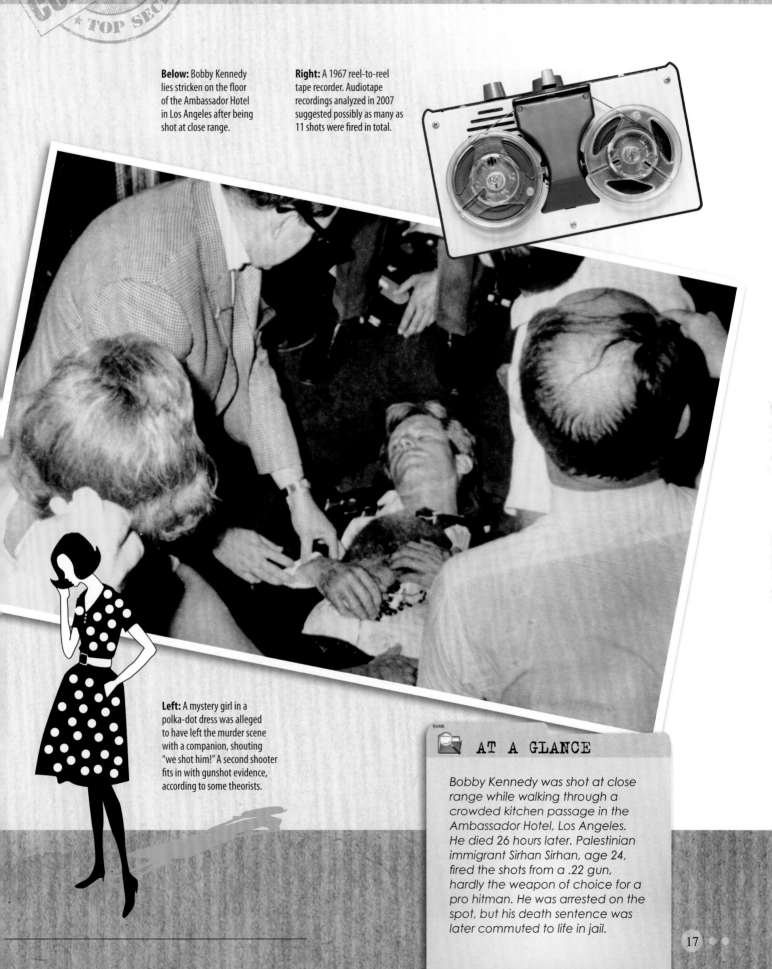

Left: A mystery girl in a polka-dot dress was alleged to have left the murder scene with a companion, shouting "we shot him!" A second shooter fits in with gunshot evidence, according to some theorists.

NAME

AT A GLANCE

Bobby Kennedy was shot at close range while walking through a crowded kitchen passage in the Ambassador Hotel, Los Angeles. He died 26 hours later. Palestinian immigrant Sirhan Sirhan, age 24, fired the shots from a .22 gun, hardly the weapon of choice for a pro hitman. He was arrested on the spot, but his death sentence was later commuted to life in jail.

KILLING CASTRO

Above: Fidel Castro in the 1960s. By then the Cuban leader had become the USA's diplomatic enemy number 1.

Below: The Northwoods Memorandum, a top secret document that sanctioned CIA acts of terrorism as a way to implicate Castro.

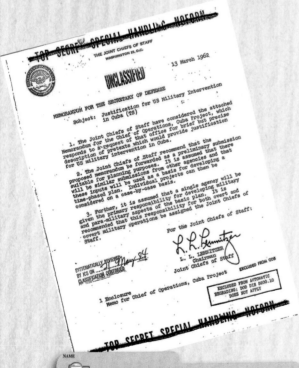

Cuba's Fidel Castro was a bogeyman to the US government, after his 1959 revolution brought communism to within a boat-ride of the United States mainland.

Cuban exiles pressed for direct action against Castro, and in 1961 President Kennedy approved the disastrous Bay of Pigs landing by exiles, backed by the CIA but without full-scale military support. The disgruntled CIA considered various schemes to get rid of Castro, such as Operation 40, which involved sabotage, and Operation Northwoods, a "false flag" conspiracy. Northwoods' plotters allegedly schemed to stage terrorist acts, such as plane hijacks and urban bombings, in the United States. They would then pin the blame on Castro, and so give the US an excuse to launch a strike on Cuba. The Northwoods planners even considered sabotaging the spaceflight by Mercury astronaut John Glenn. After CIA director Allen W. Dulles was forced to quit in 1961, President Kennedy rejected Northwoods outright.

The CIA, however, continued to plot how to neutralize, politically ruin or eliminate Castro. The "kill Castro" scenarios included using a mistress to give Castro poison pills in bed; injecting Castro "accidentally" with a poisoned pen; slipping him an exploding cigar to blow off his head; and secretly lacing his meals with chemicals to make his hair and beard fall out, thus destroying his macho revolutionary image.

Knowing Castro's fondness for scuba diving, the CIA considered offering him a contaminated wetsuit as a diplomatic gift. Wearing the toxic suit would give him a fatal disease. Another plot involved planting alluring but explosive-packed conch shells on the sea bed for Castro to pick up for his shell collection.

Castro remained an irritant to the US government, until, forced into retirement in 2008 by ill-health, he handed power to his younger brother Raul.

EVIDENCE?

The "Cuban Project" campaign by the CIA to overthrow the communist regime in Cuba was often pursued without the knowledge of the US President. At its peak, some 2,500 people were employed in anti-Castro plots! Critics lambasted the CIA for absurd and costly failure, making the United States appear "the world's biggest terrorist."

Top: Protestors in New York march for peace in 1962 during the Cuban missile crisis, when the USA and USSR came perilously close to war.

Above: Castro with cigar, in conference with his revolutionary lieutenant Ernesto "Che" Guevara. One plot scenario involved sending Castro an exploding cigar as a way to kill him.

Above: Santiago Airport in Cuba, bombed by mercenaries as part of the Bay of Pigs landing by Cuban exiles in 1961.

MARCH **APRIL 1865**

THE DEATH OF ABRAHAM LINCOLN

Abraham Lincoln, 16th President of the United States, was shot at a Washington theater on April 15, 1865. He was the first US president to be assassinated.

Lincoln is today lauded as one America's greatest presidents, but his presidency was dominated by the Civil War (1861–1865). This bloody conflict almost broke the Union and created lasting bitterness. Lincoln, a hero to the anti-slavery movement, was hated and demonized by his enemies. By the spring of 1865, the strains of leadership were clear to see. In a rare moment of relaxation, he sat down to watch a play at Ford's Theater in Washington.

Shortly after 10:00 pm, John Wilkes Booth, an actor of some repute but erratic temperament, entered the Presidential box and shot Lincoln in the head. Attempting to leap on to the stage, the assassin fell, breaking his leg. Waving a dagger and uttering Virginia's state motto "*Sic semper tyrannis*" ("Always thus to tyrants"), Booth made his getaway.

Lincoln was taken to a house nearby, but died at 7:22 next morning. Booth was tracked to a barn in Virginia and killed by Federal soldiers. His companion David Herold surrendered, and talked. Booth's accomplices were rounded up: Mary Surratt, in whose home the plot had been hatched; David Herold; George Atzerodt, a carriage-builder, and Lewis Paine, an ex-soldier. They were found guilty by a military court of conspiring to kill Lincoln, Vice President Andrew Johnson and Secretary of State William H. Seward, and all four were hanged on July 7, 1865. Samuel Arnold and Michael O'Laughlin, friends of Booth, were found guilty of helping the conspiracy and given life sentences. So too was Samuel A. Mudd, the physician who had set Booth's broken leg. Edward Spangler, a stage hand at Ford's, was jailed for six years for helping Booth escape.

EVIDENCE?

John Wilkes Booth was the younger brother of the greater actor, Edwin Thomas Booth (1833–1893). Booth's first idea was to kidnap Lincoln and hold him hostage for the release of Confederate prisoners. He seems to have decided to kill the President when news came of Robert E. Lee's surrender to Ulysses S. Grant on April 9, 1865. The South was beaten, and Lee had effectively ended the war. Booth shot Lincoln five days later.

Above: The single-shot Derringer pistol used to kill Lincoln. Easily concealed but powerful (.44 caliber) the gun is displayed at Ford's Theater Museum in Washington, DC.

Above: A contemporary and melodramatic print illustrating the shocking murder of President Lincoln by Booth. The actor-assassin entered the Presidential box and fired from point-blank range, in full view of Mrs Lincoln.

Right: Notes written by Washington city police on the night of Lincoln's assassination. The handwritten log records, at the bottom of the page, the reaction of officers to "the melancholy intelligence of the assassination of Mr Lincoln President of the US at Ford's Theater."

21

OCTOBER NOVEMBER **DECEMBER 1916**

RASPUTIN AND THE ROMANOVS

What was Rasputin's secret hold over Russia's Empress? And what really happened to the Tsar's family in 1918?

Above: Russia's imperial family: Tsar Nicholas II with the Tsarina Alexandra and their five children (from left to right): Maria (b. 1899), Alexei (b. 1904), Olga (b. 1895), Tatiana (b. 1897) and Anastasia (b. 1901).

Below: The Yusupov Palace in St Petersburg, where Prince Felix Yusupov and his fellow conspirators lured Rasputin to a violent death in 1916.

Grigori Rasputin was a Russian peasant-priest and mystic – wild-eyed, long-haired, filthy, yet able to heal the sick and bewitch high society in St Petersburg. Venerated as divinely inspired, Rasputin also had an irresistible sexual technique; he told fashionable ladies they must sin with him to gain salvation.

The Tsarina Alexandra believed Rasputin could cure her haemophiliac son Alexei, and allowed the priest familiar access to the court and family from 1905. However, as Rasputin's debauched behavior became more scandalous, and his influence more dangerous, a group of courtiers and ministers plotted to kill him. In December 1916, they first gave Rasputin poison and then shot him. Rasputin, however, clung on to life, and only eventually died when he was pushed through a hole in the ice in the River Neva, where he drowned.

Rasputin's death could not save the Russian Empire. Revolution, and Russia's near-total collapse in 1917 during the First World War, brought down the Romanov dynasty. After Lenin and the Bolsheviks took power, Tsar Nicholas II was forced to abdicate. What would happen to him and his family? Exile seemed likely, perhaps in Britain, whose King George V was the Tsar's cousin. But there was no rescue. The Tsar and Tsarina, with their five children (Alexei, Olga, Maria, Tatiana and Anastasia) were held prisoner, first outside St Petersburg and then at Ekaterinburg in the Ural Mountains. There, on July 19, 1918, they were taken to a cellar and shot. So were their doctor and three servants. The bodies were burnt and thrown down a mine-shaft.

EVIDENCE?

After the deaths of the Romanov girls, at least 10 women claimed to be the Grand Duchess Anastasia. The most persistent "pretender" was Anna Anderson, who offered some "recollections" of royal family life and had a slight physical resemblance (bunions and scars). However, DNA tests after her death in 1984 disproved any genetic tie to the Romanovs. Grand Duke Cyril, the tsar's cousin, refused to see her, and a former royal tutor said her Russian was so poor she could not possibly be the real Anastasia.

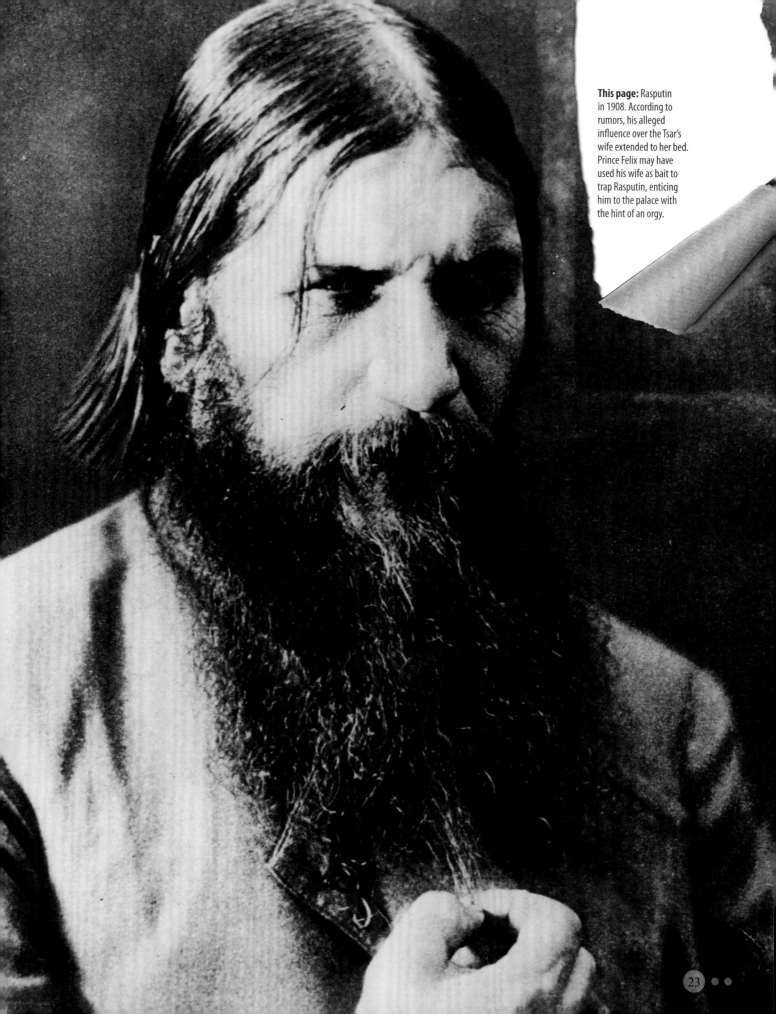

OFF SCREEN

The entertainment industry, on and off screen, feeds off fantasy and illusion. We, as audience, become willing partners in the conspiracy, believing what we see and hear. Yet, often what goes on off-screen and off-stage is stranger, and darker, than what the public sees.

The truth about Tinseltown is often tawdry, at times glaringly lit, at times shadowed by the publicity machinery. Stars of film, stage, music and television live their lives in public. Celebrities feed off the media, but they can also be devoured by it. Hollywood, in its heyday, was a cauldron of conspiracies; studio bosses plotting to steal each other's stars, the stars themselves hiding private lives and loves. While gossip columns and websites churn out stories of stars pepped by pills, drink and drugs, of sexual scandals and personal tragedies, all the while critics argue that the entertainment industry has itself become a conspiracy—to manipulate our emotions (as art does) and to shape ideas and attitudes.

APRIL MAY JUNE JULY **AUGUST 1962**

HOW DID MARILYN DIE?

On the night of August 4, 1962, the world's most famous movie star died. Was Marilyn Monroe's death an accident, suicide... or murder?

CERTIFIED COPY OF BIRTH RECORD

Above: A birth certificate said to be Monroe's. Her birth-name was either Norma Jean Baker or Norma Jean (or Jeane) Mortenson, born in Los Angeles.

Below: A 1954 magazine cover. Marilyn, then 28, had just emerged from bit-parts to starring roles in hits such as *Gentlemen Prefer Blondes* (1953).

The Los Angeles coroner's verdict was "probably suicide," resulting from a drug overdose. Aged only 36, Marilyn had come a long way from Norma Jean Baker, starlet and pin-up. Marilyn Monroe radiated superstar brilliance on and off the screen. Her private life was complicated, her marriages to baseball hero Joe Di Maggio and playwright Arthur Miller front-page news. Secret lovers included President John F. Kennedy.

Off-screen, Monroe was deeply insecure, unable to sleep without pills, addicted to barbiturates, and heavily reliant on psychoanalysis. Suicide or accidental overdose seemed feasible causes for her death, but fans, theorists and some Monroe biographers conjured scenarios in which she was killed by a barbiturates enema that reacted fatally with the cocktail of other medication. The most lurid version has Mafia hit-men forcibly administering the rectal dose.

Monroe's frailty and potential for indiscretion was, it's claimed, a threat to the Kennedys. Both John and Bobby had reportedly been Marilyn's lovers, while hovering in the shadows was Mafia boss Sam Giancana. One version of her death blames agents, either working for the Kennedys (to eliminate Marilyn as a danger) or paid by the Mafia or the CIA to enmesh the Kennedys in a murder and so wreck their political careers. It was hard for Monroe's millions of fans to accept that this icon of glamor, albeit often a tragic figure, could have played her last scene face-down on a bed in her bungalow with a bottle of sleeping pills on the bedside table. More comforting surely to imagine her as innocent victim, used, abused and finally discarded by the powerful men she had beguiled, but for whom she had become a liability.

Focus 10¢ MARCH

The END of MARILYN MONROE

HARLEM CONFIDENTIAL: IS IT LICKING ITS TEEN-AGE DOPE?

EVIDENCE?

Hundreds of books have been written about Marilyn Monroe, some with tales of "secret tapes" and "private diaries" claiming to reveal the hidden truth. The more likely reality is that her death was a tragic accident. She went to bed at 8:00 pm, having at 5:15 pm called her doctor Ralph Greenson about her sleeping problem. At 3:00 am, Eunice Murray, her housekeeper, seeing the light still on, found the body.

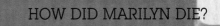

Above: A typical Monroe publicity photo – the sex-goddess of 1950s Hollywood. She made 28 films in a career that began in 1948 with the film *Dangerous Years* – an ominous title perhaps.

Right: Marilyn Monroe's star on Hollywood's Walk of Fame. Her beauty, life and death made her one of the most written-about movie stars of all time.

APRIL MAY JUNE JULY AUGUST 1977

ELVIS LIVES!

Fans often cannot accept that their rock idols are mortal, so they come up with strange theories to explain their sudden passing.

The untimely death, at the age of 42, of Elvis Aaron Presley on August 16, 1977, seemed sadly inevitable. "The King" of rock 'n' roll had become a caricature of his former self, bloated by ill-health, drug abuse and over-eating. His death from a drugs overdose (largely antidepressants and sleeping pills) was widely mourned by his fans, and his place in the pop pantheon assured.

Among his many fans were some who simply denied that Elvis was dead, despite the fact that after his death his body had lain in an open casket at Graceland for his fans to file past. "No, Elvis lives!" was the cry, and reports of Elvis sightings continued for years. Conspiracists claim he was a secret agent working for the FBI and US anti-narcotics agencies, his "death" faked to protect him from vengeance-seeking drug cartels and give him a new identity.

Above: Two tickets for the concert Presley never played, dated August 19, 1977. Elvis died three days earlier. Or had he actually, as some conspiracy theorists claim, simply taken himself off to the backwoods, out of the limelight?

Below: Elvis the King in full swing, on tour in April 1972 – no longer the slim youth of the 1950s, but still rocking.

Rumors have followed the deaths of other pop heroes, too: Brian Jones of The Rolling Stones (dead in a swimming pool), Jim Morrison of The Doors (drug overdose, murder, not dead at all?), Jimi Hendrix (choked on vomit, suicide, murder?) and Michael Jackson (drugs, but how induced?).

How John Lennon died seemed more clear. In 1980, the former Beatle, aged 40, was shot in New York City by Mark Chapman, a deranged fan who had earlier been given Lennon's autograph. Fellow-Beatle George Harrison survived a knife attack in 1999, fighting off his assailant with a poker, but died from cancer in 2001. Paul McCartney was rumored to have "died" in 1966, in a car accident, and been replaced by a double. Was there a clue in the song Revolution 9? Played backward, some people claim the sound of a car crash can be heard, and the words "turn me on, dead man." Paul went on performing, however, and most people give no more than a second's consideration to this most bizarre of theories.

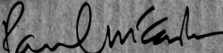

Left: A British stamp reproducing the Beatles *Abbey Road* album cover, an image that has intrigued some conspiracy theorists.

Top: The Dakota apartment building in New York City, corner of 72nd and Central Park West in Upper West Side, Manhattan. John Lennon lived here and was shot at the entrance to the building.

Above: The unfired 6th bullet from Mark Chapman's gun, test-fired to provide evidence at his trial for the murder of John Lennon. The bullet was later presented by the New York police to the Metropolitan Police Museum.

NAME

EVIDENCE?

Chapman's confused explanations for shooting Lennon involved J.D. Salinger's novel The Catcher in the Rye, and a belief that Lennon claimed to be more important than Jesus. Chapman apparently contemplated killing Elizabeth Taylor or Jackie Kennedy Onassis, but Lennon was easier to find. Chapman killed him with five bullets.

1930s–TODAY

Above: Early horror movies created fantasies about aliens and oversized dinosaurs that played on the American audience's fears of Communist threats and nuclear war.

Below: Science fiction movies offer vehicles for environmental or political messages—and may encourage some people to think that aliens from outer space are already here!

HOLLYWOOD INFLUENCE

Good or bad, movies certainly influence us, and movie stars become role models. Is this just how art works, or do movie-makers set out to deliberately change our perceptions and attitudes—not always for the best?

Conspiracy theorists argue that ever since the first movies flickered on screen in the early 1900s, some moviemakers have used their huge power at the behest of their paymasters. Science fiction films of the 1950s were made to downplay the existence of real UFOs and aliens, and/or to harden attitudes toward the Soviet Union and China. Some claim that "Mob-money" shapes movie output, that Disney's *Fantasia* is full of references to Illuminati black magic, that Errol Flynn was a Nazi sympathizer (in fact he was inclined to the left), that the CIA killed James Dean because he was a leader of teenage rebellion, and, famously, that Stanley Kubrick directed the Apollo Moon landings. Certainly moviemaking is seldom free of intrigue, and a fair bit of double-dealing, and the line between art and propaganda can be thin. Around the world, moviemakers are routinely used by governments for propaganda, as pioneered by Nazi lies-spinner Josef Goebbels in the 1930s.

AT A GLANCE

Hollywood has cashed in on, and fed, the public appetite for conspiracy through a string of hit movies over the years. Examples are JFK (the Kennedy killing); All the President's Men (Watergate); The Boys from Brazil (Nazis hiding away in South America); The Day of the Jackal (the plot to assassinate French leader Charles de Gaulle) and the Bourne films (don't trust anyone!).

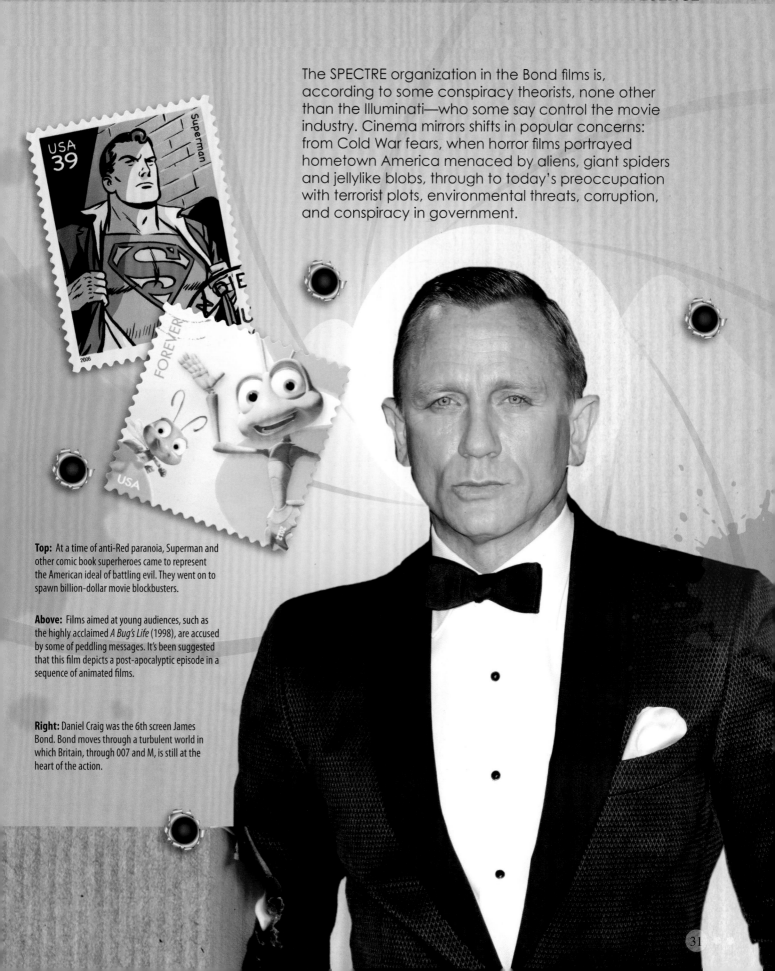

The SPECTRE organization in the Bond films is, according to some conspiracy theorists, none other than the Illuminati—who some say control the movie industry. Cinema mirrors shifts in popular concerns: from Cold War fears, when horror films portrayed hometown America menaced by aliens, giant spiders and jellylike blobs, through to today's preoccupation with terrorist plots, environmental threats, corruption, and conspiracy in government.

Top: At a time of anti-Red paranoia, Superman and other comic book superheroes came to represent the American ideal of battling evil. They went on to spawn billion-dollar movie blockbusters.

Above: Films aimed at young audiences, such as the highly acclaimed *A Bug's Life* (1998), are accused by some of peddling messages. It's been suggested that this film depicts a post-apocalyptic episode in a sequence of animated films.

Right: Daniel Craig was the 6th screen James Bond. Bond moves through a turbulent world in which Britain, through 007 and M, is still at the heart of the action.

ROYAL MURDER

The history of the world is strewn with murdered monarchs, an A to Z of regicide from Abdullah of Jordan to Xerxes of Persia.

Julius Caesar fell victim to one of the most famous historical conspiracies, and later Roman emperors and their families were especially vulnerable, plotting to kill one another or being eliminated by poison, strangling or knife. Some kings died fighting, such as Richard III of England, killed at Bosworth in 1485 by a conspiratorial Tudor rival, who became King Henry VII. Others fell victim to dark conspiracies: William Rufus, King of England, was shot by an unseen bowman; Lord Darnley, husband of Mary Queen of Scots, was blown up and then strangled for good measure. Many kings and queens lived in daily fear of murder—Elizabeth I of England survived assassins' plots, and several would-be killers tried to remove Queen Victoria. Uneasy lay the head that wore a crown indeed.

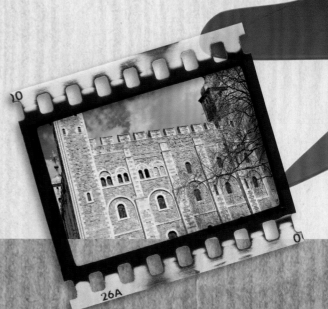

FEBRUARY MARCH **APRIL 1483**

MURDERED MONARCHS

"Uneasy lies the head that wears a crown..." wrote Shakespeare, and the chronicle of murdered monarchs makes grisly reading.

Above: The Tower of London, where, in 1583, the two Yorkist princes were probably murdered. What is now known as the Bloody Tower was at the time called the Garden Tower.

Below: The coat of arms of Richard III. He was blamed by Henry Tudor's supporters (and later Shakespeare) for the murder of the two young princes in the tower.

Kings make enemies, and many kings have met violent deaths, either in battle or by an assassin's hand. Mystery surrounds the death in 1100 of William Rufus, son of the Norman William the Conqueror. He was shot while out hunting. But was it an accident or did the bowman have the king in full view as he drew back the bowstring? Walter Tirel was named as the culprit, but only much later.

When England's King Edward IV died, naturally, in April 1483, his son should have been crowned Edward V. However, an uncle stood in his path – and so arose the story of the Princes in the Tower. Edward V, who was only 12 years old, was taken in charge by his mother and her unpopular Woodville relatives, but decoyed away by their uncle Richard of Gloucester. He persuaded the queen to hand over both Edward and his younger brother Richard. Both boys were shut up in the Tower of London and declared illegitimate, and Richard became King Richard III in July 1483.

The two princes were glimpsed in the Tower, but by summer's end were never seen again. Richard ruled until 1485, when he lost the Battle of Bosworth to Henry Tudor, who made himself Henry VII.

Oddly, one name recurs in the stories of these deaths 400 years apart: Tirel/Tyrell. Tudor historians blamed Sir James Tyrrel as the Princes' chief assassin. Bones were found in a chest in the Tower in 1674 and buried in Westminster Abbey, but without DNA testing, no proof exists that they are those of Edward V and his brother Richard, Duke of York.

NAME

📁 AT A GLANCE

Some historians claim the young princes in the tower were given new identities, protected by Henry VII and Elizabeth Woodville. One version suggests that Edward V died of natural causes, while Richard lived in obscurity as a bricklayer in Essex. More certain is that the Tudors fought off "pretenders," the most threatening being Perkin Warbeck, a Flemish jack-the-lad who claimed he was Prince Richard. After trying to escape from the Tower, he was hanged in 1499.

Above: William Rufus lies dead in the New Forest. Walter Tirel is seen here riding away, but whether he is a murderer fleeing or a subject riding to fetch help after a tragic accident is not known.

FEBRUARY MARCH APRIL | MAY 1536

HEADS ON THE BLOCK

The Tower of London has been the last earthly abode for many prisoners doomed to die on the block by the sword or the ax.

Henry VIII's reign saw a steady flow of noble prisoners into the Tower, often through the river entrance known then as the watergate, but today known as Traitors' Gate. Thomas More was beheaded on Tower Hill in 1535 for refusing to acknowledge the King as head of the English Church. Within a year, Henry's second wife, the bewitching Anne Boleyn, had also been beheaded – executed at her request by a French swordsman. Her "crime" was betraying the King by her adultery, supposedly with five men, who were all executed, too. Evidence hardly counted in the face of Henry's rage and frustration at Anne's failure to give him a healthy son (she had only borne him a daughter, the future Queen Elizabeth I). Yet Anne was almost certainly innocent, at least of adultery with the men named at the times and places set out in her indictment.

In 1542 Catherine Howard, fifth wife of Henry VIII, was also beheaded for adultery. Beside her died Jane Boleyn, Lady Rochford, her "accomplice." Henry VIII's court was riven by feuds between the Seymours (the brothers of his third wife, Jane Seymour) and the Howards. Another Howard, the Early of Surrey, was executed in 1547, when Henry became convinced that Howard had planned to usurp the crown from his son, the future Edward VI.

Thomas Seymour was executed in 1549, his brother Edward in 1552. When sickly Edward VI died in 1553, the Duke of Northumberland tried to make his daughter-in-law Lady Jane Grey queen, usurping Henry's daughters, the princesses Mary and Elizabeth. After nine days, Mary's supporters won the power-struggle, and 14-year-old Lady Jane, an innocent, was told by her father Suffolk she was no longer queen. In February 1554 she and her husband were executed. Suffolk and Northumberland soon followed them to the block.

Top: Anne Boleyn, second wife of King Henry VIII. She was executed in 1536 for treason, including adultery. She asked to be beheaded by a swordsman.

Above: Prisoners who entered the Tower by the watergate seldom came out alive. One who did was Anne Boleyn's daughter, Elizabeth, in the reign of her half-sister Mary I.

CASE CLOSED

Left: The executioner's ax did not always sever a head with one blow. The execution of Lady Salisbury in 1541 reportedly needed 11 blows.

Below: A coin (a half-groat) from the reign of Henry VIII. The condemned usually paid their executioner out of their own pocket, as well as forgiving him in advance for his actions.

Above: Lady Jane Grey blindfolded before the block. Made queen by her scheming father-in-law, the blameless Jane was beheaded on February 12, 1554, after being the "uncrowned" queen of England for nine days.

NAME

📁 **AT A GLANCE**

Elizabeth I, as a 21-year-old princess, passed through Traitors' Gate in 1554, fearful of the same fate as her mother Anne Boleyn. She was suspected of conspiring with Sir Thomas Wyatt against Queen Mary I (her half-sister). Wyatt swore she was innocent, before he was beheaded, and Elizabeth was released from the Tower.

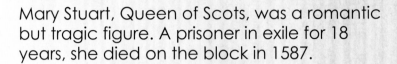

TRAGIC MARY

Mary Stuart, Queen of Scots, was a romantic but tragic figure. A prisoner in exile for 18 years, she died on the block in 1587.

Just before her execution Mary remarked to an attendant, "Did I not tell you this would happen? I knew they would never allow me to live..." She believed her Catholic faith caused her downfall, though politics as much as religion caused Mary's head to roll.

Mary became Queen of Scotland in 1542, as a baby, after her father James V died broken-hearted at defeat by the English. Mary was raised in France and married the heir to the French throne, becoming Queen of France in 1559. But when her husband Francis died the following year, she returned to Scotland, a land she barely knew, with its prating Protestant clerics and feuding nobles. In 1565 Mary married her cousin, Lord Darnley, a Catholic who was related to the royal Tudors. By 1566 she was pregnant, but already out of love, for in a vicious act of jealousy and rage, Darnley had had her secretary, David Rizzio, stabbed to death. By the time Mary gave birth to her son James in June 1566, she may already have found a new love in James Hepburn, Earl of Bothwell.

Then, on the night of February 10, 1567, a sensational murder enveloped Mary in scandal. A house in Edinburgh was blown up by gunpowder, the blast waking Mary in Holyrood House. Her husband Darnley was found dead in the garden, strangled. On May 15, Mary married Bothwell. Her reputation was in tatters. Had she conspired to murder Darnley? Was she a willing bride, or a woman "ravished" by a brutal abductor? The Scots nobles turned against her, and forced her to abdicate in favor of her son.

Left: Queen Elizabeth I of England and Mary shared a royal ancestor: King Henry VII, founder of the Tudor line. He was Elizabeth's grandfather and Mary's great-grandfather.

Below: Holyrood House in Edinburgh is where Mary's secretary Rizzio was murdered. Queen Victoria asked to see the murder-room on her first visit in 1850, and was shown bloodstains on the floor.

AT A GLANCE

NAME

Mary's claim to the English throne was through her grandmother, Margaret Tudor, sister of Henry VIII. Mary succeeded her father James V in Scotland, in 1542. Henry died in 1547. After Henry came his son Edward VI, his elder daughter Mary I, and then Elizabeth I in 1558. So long as Elizabeth remained childless, Mary was next in line, but in the end, her son James took her place in both Scotland and England.

Above: Mary Stuart, Queen of Scots. When she left France for her native Scotland, she was plunged into a world of conspiracy, jealousy and religious fanaticism.

DECEMBER JANUARY FEBRUARY 1587

Mary then fled to England, where her cousin Queen Elizabeth I, ambivalent as always, kept her a prisoner for 18 years. Elizabeth was unwilling to send Mary back to possible death in Scotland at the hands of her enemies, but was also fearful of Catholic-inspired plots in England, encouraged by France or Spain. It suited her, and her government, to have the infant James on the throne of Scotland rather than the potentially meddlesome Mary. In 1570, fears of plots were increased when the Pope excommunicated Elizabeth (outlawing her from the Catholic Church) and sanctioned her removal.

Above: The death of David Rizzio, Italian secretary and card-partner of Mary Queen of Scots. Mary's husband Darnley planned and supervised the brutal slaying by multiple stab wounds.

Left: Queen Elizabeth confers with her spymaster, Sir Francis Walsingham. His agents and informers trapped Mary into her fatal involvement in the Babington Plot, a conspiracy that Walsingham covertly managed.

Right: The signed document from England's Privy Council ordering the execution of Mary Queen of Scots after her trial in October 1586. Her son James made no move or appeal to save her life.

In the middle of the web of intrigue sat Elizabeth's spymaster, Sir Francis Walsingham, whose agents set up a cipher code system to monitor a fatal plot, exposed in 1586. Antony Babington led a hot-headed Catholic conspiracy to kill Elizabeth, bring in foreign soldiers, and make Mary queen. Letters between Mary and the Babington plotters went straight to Walsingham, sealing Mary's fate. Elizabeth signed the death warrant (afterward denying she'd done so), and Mary was executed on February 8, 1587. The executioner needed two blows to sever Mary's head, which caused her wig to fall off. Her clothes were burned, to leave no relics.

NAME

EVIDENCE

After Darnley's murder, Mary was lampooned in Scottish scandal-sheets as a whore. Few people believed the "abduction" story, deciding that she had run off willingly with Bothwell, who later deserted her.

Above: Mary protests her innocence when shown the warrant for her execution. Told she would die the following morning, she said it was welcome news for "I am very glad to go…"

AUGUST SEPTEMBER OCTOBER

Above: Following torture on the rack, Guy Fawkes eventually revealed the names of his fellow-conspirators. This is his statement, made under duress, the signature that of a broken man. He went to the gallows in January 1606.

NAME

EVIDENCE

After his arrest, Fawkes kept silent for two days, but racked in agony under torture he finally gasped out the names of the other conspirators. Catesby and the others had fled London and ended up at Holbeach House in the Midlands, where they were trapped by 200 soldiers. Trying to dry out damp gunpowder, they caused an explosive fire that blinded one of them. In the fight that followed, Catesby and a few of the others were killed. The rest were dragged away for trial and execution at the gallows.

NOVEMBER 1605

THE GUNPOWDER PLOT

Guy Fawkes tried to blow up the Houses of Parliament—as most people know, but behind the familiar story lies an unsolved mystery.

Guy Fawkes, born in York in 1570, was a Catholic in a Protestant kingdom. English Catholics hoped that James I, who succeeded Elizabeth I in 1603, would do away with some of the many laws that discriminated against Catholics. When these hopes were dashed, Fawkes joined a conspiracy led by Robert Catesby. The conspirators' radical plan involved blowing up the Houses of Parliament, killing or scaring away the king, and putting his daughter Elizabeth on the throne with a Catholic husband.

By late 1605 there were 13 conspirators. The chosen "bomber" was Guy Fawkes, who knew something about gunpowder from his days as a soldier. Using the name John Johnson, he took a rented house close to the Palace of Westminster and stacked its cellar with 36 barrels of gunpowder, rowed across the Thames from Catesby's house in Lambeth. On the evening of November 4, 1605, Fawkes hid in the cellar and waited.

What Fawkes didn't know was that the plotters had already been betrayed. On October 26, Lord Monteagle received an anonymous letter warning him to stay away from Parliament on November 5. Monteagle took the letter to Robert Cecil, chief minister, and Cecil told King James. The king ordered a search of Parliament and the surrounding buildings. At first the searchers ignored a "tall man" beside a stack of firewood (a servant, perhaps?). But about midnight, a second search party arrested "a very tall and desperate fellow," who was Guy Fawkes. Catesby and the others fled. Some were killed resisting arrest and the others, including Fawkes, were hanged.

The plot was more bad news for Catholics, and who wrote the letter to Lord Monteagle remains a mystery.

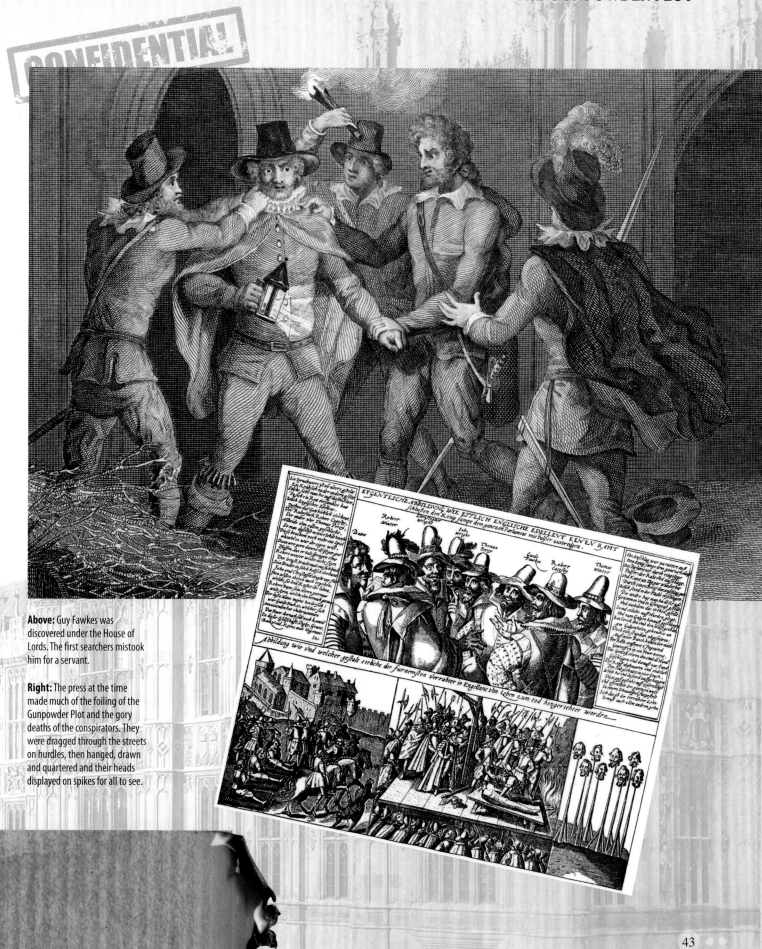

CONFIDENTIAL

Above: Guy Fawkes was discovered under the House of Lords. The first searchers mistook him for a servant.

Right: The press at the time made much of the foiling of the Gunpowder Plot and the gory deaths of the conspirators. They were dragged through the streets on hurdles, then hanged, drawn and quartered and their heads displayed on spikes for all to see.

OUT OF THIS WORLD

Are we alone, or has the future already arrived in an alien spacecraft? Most conspiracy theories have their roots in the belief that controlling forces, usually governments or quasi-government bodies, are pulling the strings.

However, a mass of speculation suggests that the conspiracy is literally out of this world—that aliens have been visiting Earth for thousands of years, are still doing so, and have secret contacts with government. It's alleged that real spacecraft, dead aliens, and even live real-life ETs, are hidden away at secret locations. Just as astounding is the suggestion that Neil Armstrong's historic first Moon-step in 1969 never happened, since the Apollo landing was a fake—a front for one of the most audacious cons of all time. If we can believe that astronauts went no farther than Hollywood, the cosmos must be a far madder place than any scriptwriter ever conceived!

MARCH APRIL MAY JUNE JULY 1947

THE ROSWELL INCIDENT

Probably the most-discussed "alien landing" incident was in 1947. Did aliens die in the desert of New Mexico?

In July 1947, a rancher in Roswell, New Mexico, USA, found metal debris on the ground. Was it a plane crash, or something other-worldly? America was gripped by "flying saucer fever," and the local newspaper headlined the startling news that the military had "captured a flying saucer." A press release mentioning a "flying disk" was swiftly dismissed with a counter-statement that the debris came from a weather balloon that had met with a mishap.

The balloon story, though, seemed to some to be a clumsy cover-up for a more fantastic truth. Not only had an alien spacecraft crashed, but its alien crew had been recovered and spirited away. Witnesses spoke of gouges in the desert, made by a craft crashing, and UFO-converts speculated that military radar signals had messed up the alien craft's control systems. The Roswell aliens became part of UFO-mythology, with a mortician claiming to have helped with post-mortems, and in 1995 a video clip on the Internet showing the actual "autopsy" of a Roswell alien—a humanoid biped of the kind known in extraterrestrial-watching circles as a "gray."

Above: Khrushchev and Kennedy meet in the 1960s. Both sides claimed the other was testing secret weapons.

Below: This 1956 UFO book advertisement suggests that UFO witnesses had been gagged by the authorities.

WANTED
FOR
TREASON

THIS MAN is wanted for treasonous activities against the United States:

1. Betraying the Constitution (which he swore to uphold): He is turning the sovereignty of the U.S. over to the communist controlled United Nations. He is betraying our friends (Cuba, Katanga, Portugal) and befriending our enemies (Russia, Yugoslavia, Poland).
2. He has been WRONG on innumerable issues affecting the security of the U.S. (United Nations-Berlin wall-Missle removal-Cuba-Wheat deals-Test Ban Treaty, etc.)
3. He has been lax in enforcing Communist Registration laws.
4. He has given support and encouragement to the Communist inspired racial riots.
5. He has illegally invaded a sovereign State with federal troops.
6. He has consistantly appointed Anti-Christians to Federal office: Upholds the Supreme Court in its Anti-Christian rulings. Aliens and known Communists abound in Federal offices.
7. He has been caught in fantastic LIES to the American people (including personal ones like his previous marriage and divorce).

EVIDENCE?

NAME

Conspiracy theorists were excited by a memo released in 2011 under US Freedom of Information law. Sent in March 1950 by an FBI agent, it claimed "three so-called flying saucers had been recovered," each with three bodies "of human shape but only [0.9 m] 3 feet tall" and wearing pressure suits. This memo might seem to shorten the odds on the Roswell aliens being real, but it's almost certainly a hoax.

SUSPECT

The authorities were adamant: there was no Roswell space crash and no alien corpses being preserved under guard in military freezers. The US Air Force insists to this day that there is "absolutely no evidence that a spaceship crashed near Roswell" or that any dead aliens were recovered.

Over the years more ufologists have come, albeit reluctantly, to share this view. The available evidence, much of it based on hearsay and fading memories, points to a negative: no close encounter, this time. This has not, however, stopped the Roswell Incident from entering UFO folklore and from being an ongoing inspiration for creative writers and film-makers. Nothing beats a dead alien, except, of course, a live one…

Right: A sign likely to invite the curious rather than send them off in the opposite direction. A surprisingly large number of people still believe aliens have landed.

Below: Irving Newton, a weatherman at Roswell Army Air Field, New Mexico, holds up debris from the supposed flying saucer found at the Roswell crash site (top).

Left: Anti-Kennedy propaganda. The President was killed in 1963, according to some conspiracy theorists, to stop him revealing to the world the "Big Lie"—that Roswell really happened, the US government had covered up the presence of aliens, and that there was a secret world government.

MARCH APRIL MAY JUNE 1947

THE GREAT UFO COVER-UP

Projects Sign, Grunge, Blue Book; were these cover-names to hide the amazing truth, that UFOs were indeed from outer space?

In 1947, pilot Kenneth Arnold helped ignite the modern UFO (Unidentified Flying Object) controversy. While flying near Mt Rainier in Washington state, USA, he saw nine flying disks, each "like a saucer skipping across a lake." The name stuck and became widely used. Arnold wondered if he'd seen alien spacecraft, but sceptics argue it was a meteoroid breaking up, making fireballs in the atmosphere.

That same year the pilots of a US DC-3 airliner spotted a strange craft "with two rows of windows" spitting flames from its tail. In 1948 Captain Thomas Mantell crashed in his P-51 Mustang while pursuing a mysterious object. The US Air Force said he had chased after the planet Venus and met with a tragic accident, but ufologists argued that the unlucky pilot had tangled with an alien. In 1950, in his book *Flying Saucers are Real*, Donald Keyhoe speculated that UFOs were probably extraterrestrial, had been visiting Earth for centuries, and seemed peaceful. A typical "sighting" was in 1964, when Lonnie Zamora, a policeman in Socorro, New Mexico, saw two small "aliens" who then took off in their oval spacecraft. Witnesses said their "aliens" were like small people, with long arms and large heads—no bug-eyed monsters or giant blobs. When shot at by gun-happy farmers, "aliens" somersaulted or floated away unharmed.

Left: A Swedish air force officer conducts a search for a "ghost rocket" reported crashing in Lake Kolmjarv, Sweden, in July 1946. Could ghost rockets be UFOs? Meteors? Or Soviet missiles going astray?

Above: Top secret, this 1948 US Air Force document (declassified in 1997) suggested that some experts regarded the ghost rocket evidence as possibly indicating extraterrestrial origins.

Below: The mystery plane that officially does not exist: the US SR-91 Aurora.

EVIDENCE?

"Pilots have continued reporting unexplained "sightings." In 2008 a police helicopter near Cardiff almost collided with a mystery craft, which it chased as far as north Devon. The official line remains the same: no evidence that UFOs are extraterrestrial in origin. In 2009 it was suggested a secret US spy plane named Aurora, which officially does not exist, might be the origin of at least some UFO sightings."

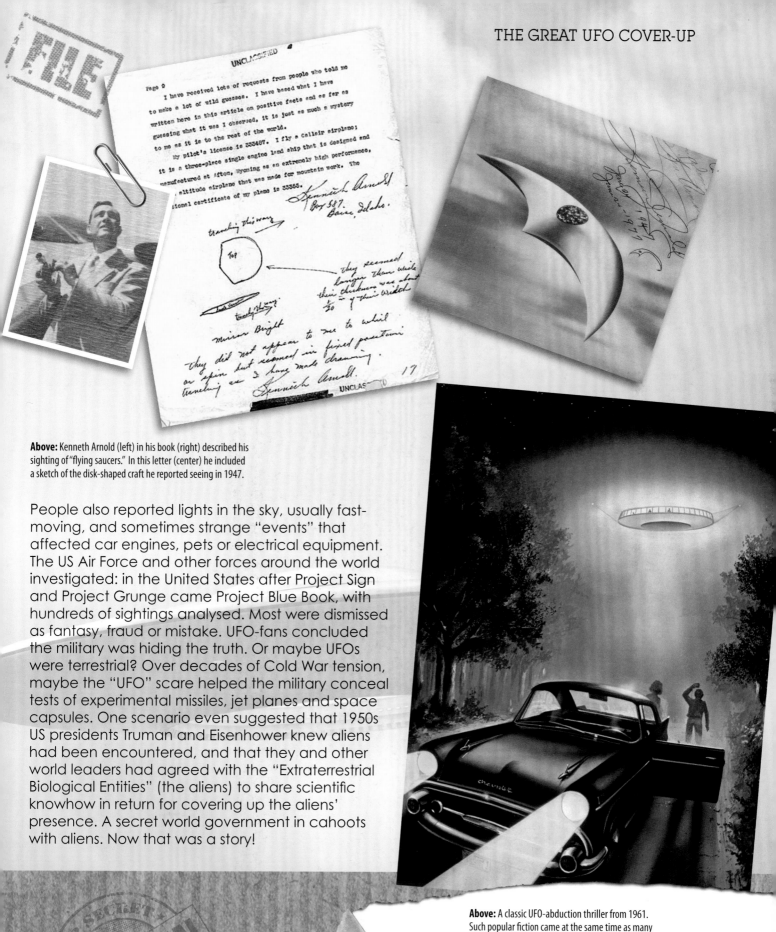

Above: Kenneth Arnold (left) in his book (right) described his sighting of "flying saucers." In this letter (center) he included a sketch of the disk-shaped craft he reported seeing in 1947.

People also reported lights in the sky, usually fast-moving, and sometimes strange "events" that affected car engines, pets or electrical equipment. The US Air Force and other forces around the world investigated: in the United States after Project Sign and Project Grunge came Project Blue Book, with hundreds of sightings analysed. Most were dismissed as fantasy, fraud or mistake. UFO-fans concluded the military was hiding the truth. Or maybe UFOs were terrestrial? Over decades of Cold War tension, maybe the "UFO" scare helped the military conceal tests of experimental missiles, jet planes and space capsules. One scenario even suggested that 1950s US presidents Truman and Eisenhower knew aliens had been encountered, and that they and other world leaders had agreed with the "Extraterrestrial Biological Entities" (the aliens) to share scientific knowhow in return for covering up the aliens' presence. A secret world government in cahoots with aliens. Now that was a story!

Above: A classic UFO-abduction thriller from 1961. Such popular fiction came at the same time as many conspiracy theories regarding alien craft.

MARCH APRIL MAY JUNE 1950-1960s

HAVE ALIENS WALKED ON EARTH?

Did extraterrestrials visit Earth in ancient times? Science says not. But ET-theorists point to "evidence" from antiquity as well as more recent close encounters.

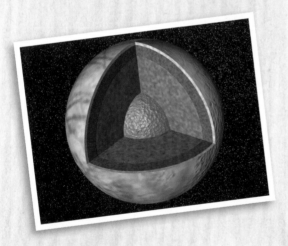

Above: Carl Sagan with a model of the Viking lander that visited Mars in 1976. Subsequent landings have failed to provide clear evidence of life on Mars—though some conspiracy theorists claim positive findings have been concealed.

Below: Jupiter's 4th largest moon, Europa, shown in cutaway. It is possible Europa had oceans in its past and maybe still has liquid water trapped beneath thick ice on its surface, and so perhaps life-forms, too.

Supporters of the "aliens came here long ago" theory point to ancient stories of gods flying in fiery chariots, and to pictures of ancient rulers in strange garb and headdress, said to be aliens in spacesuits. Extraterrestrial visitors arrived with advanced technology to observe Earth, and perhaps genetically modify its life-forms. They helpfully passed on some basic technology—such as teaching the Sumerians agriculture and maths. They also helped build the pyramids and Stonehenge.

This theory presupposes that intelligent life exists elsewhere in the universe. In the 1960s, astrophysicists I. S. Shklovski and Carl Sagan, serious scientists, and essentially sceptics, judged that extraterrestrials were "possible but not proven." Erich Von Daniken on the other hand claimed much "evidence" for alien visitors in the art, religion and folklore of many cultures. Zecharia Sitchkin went further, suggesting aliens produced modern humans: from a distant planet called Nibiru they flew to Earth for minerals, and genetically engineered the primitive primates they found here to make intelligent workers. When the aliens left discomfited by natural disasters and the last Ice Age, humans took over.

In 1952 George Adamski said he met a man from Venus in the Colorado Desert of California. The alien, who had long blonde hair, used telepathy to talk to Adamski, and invited him on a trip to Venus in his flying saucer. Adamski was not alone; others too claim to have met aliens, who visit from planets near and far.

NAME

EVIDENCE

Scientists believe Venus to be hostile to life, though Adamski claimed his Venusians lived safely underground. Adamski did not believe the first-ever photos of the barren far side of the Moon, taken in 1959 by a Soviet spacecraft, saying they'd been faked to hide the alien cities that were really there. Life of some kind might exist on Mars, but bacteria are unlikely to be up to building spacecraft to visit Earth!

Left: This is what a "scout craft" from Venus looked like, according to George Adamski, who claimed he met visitors from Venus in the 1950s.

Below: The Pyramids of Egypt and the ancient stones at Stonehenge in England. Are these marvels of human ingenuity in a pre-machine age, or could they be evidence that aliens arrived to "engineer" human civilization?

SUSPECT

AREA 51

A few outbuildings in the dusty Nevada desert may conceal an amazing truth—that alien visitors not only came to Earth, but are still here. Or maybe they were not aliens at all, but creatures from the future!

Area 51 has been a magnet for conspiracy theories ever since the "flying saucer" sensations of the 1940s and 50s. Even today, visiting TV crews driving along the dirt road from nearby Rachel can find themselves suddenly confronted by armed guards, who make it clear that no visitors are allowed—no trespassing, no photos permitted. In 1947 the "Roswell incident" started a long-running conspiracy theory. Lieutenant Walter Haut, base PR man at the time, put out a release explaining that the "crashed spacecraft" was just a weather balloon. But when Haut died in 2006, he left an affidavit confirming what ufologists had long claimed, that the "balloon" was a cover-story and that aliens had landed, been studied at Area 51, and were even still at Area 51. In 1987 Robert Lazar claimed that alien spacecraft were being studied, and copied by reverse engineering, at an Area 51 facility known as S-4; his claims were ridiculed, along with his credibility—but that simply added more fuel to the conspiracy fire.

Above: This map shows the site of Area 51, and the Nellis Air Force Range. The location in the Nevada desert is about as discouraging to visitors as any secret operation could wish for.

Above: The US Air Force test hi-tech aircraft, such as this 1960s YF-12A, over Area 51.

Left: According to microbiologist Dan Burisch, an alien creature similar to these is housed in an underground laboratory at S-4/Area 51. It is called "J-Rod", and it came from a distant star-system.

NAME

THE TRUTH?

Is Area 51 just a collection of huts, or a time-portal? Area 51 scientist Dan Burisch claimed to have seen an alien called "J-Rod", who is telepathic, comes from 50,000 years in the future, needs medical attention, and is here to recover genetic material to repair biological damage to our descendants. A mind-blowing idea…

Below: Area 51, close to Groom Lake and Papoose Lake, looks deserted, but any visitors are confronted by signs that warn them to keep out.

WARNING
AREA 51
Restricted Area

It is unlawful to enter this area without permission of the Installation Commander.
Sec.21, International Security Act of 1950; 50 U.S.C.797

While on this installation all personnel and the property under their control are subject to search.

USE OF DEADLY FORCE AUTHORIZED
AREA 51

OFFICIAL WHITE HOUSE RESPONSE TO
formally acknowledge an extraterrestrial presence engaging the human race - Disclosure, and 1 other petition

Searching for ET, But No Evidence Yet

Left: Attempts to find extraterrestrials include (1) the Kepler spacecraft, searching for Earthlike planets; (2) the Allen Array in California, listening for signals from deep space; and (3) robot explorers such as the *Curiosity* rover on Mars.

Right: A letter from the US Air Force denies that Area 51 even exists, but confirms that things go on in the desert that cannot be disclosed because they are classified.

DEPARTMENT OF THE AIR FORCE
WASHINGTON DC 20330-1000

Office of the Secretary

AUG 1998

Dear

This responds to your letter to the Secretary of the Air Force regarding "Area 51."

Neither the Air Force nor the Department of Defense owns or operates any location known as "Area 51." There are a variety of activities, some of which are classified, throughout what is often called the Air Force's Nellis Range Complex. There is an operating location near Groom Dry Lake. Specific activities and operations conducted on the Nellis Range, both past and present, remain classified and cannot be discussed publicly.

We hope this information is helpful.

Sincerely

JEFFREY A. RAMMES, Major, USAF
Chief, White House Inquiry Branch
Office of Legislative Liaison

TOP SECRET
CONFIDENTIAL

53

JULY 1969

MOON LANDING

"Houston, Tranquility Base here. The Eagle has landed." Millions of people around the world listened and watched on TV as US astronaut Neil Armstrong stepped down on to the surface of the Moon. But had the *Eagle* really landed on the Moon—or on a film set?

Sceptics suggest the Moon landing never happened. They claim that after technical problems threatened the project, NASA staged an elaborate hoax in great secrecy to fulfil President Kennedy's 1961 vow to Congress. Kennedy had called for the United States to commit know-how, manpower and limitless cash to "landing a man on the Moon and returning him safely to Earth" before the decade was over. Given the risks of a spaceflight beyond Earth orbit, sceptics argue, it was safer to win the space race by deception. It was important not to fail, to beat the Russians and to distract the US public from the unpopular Vietnam War.

Conspiracy theorists point to apparent anomalies on the film footage of the Apollo astronauts, such as "camera crosshairs" on Moon rocks, the Stars and Stripes flag seemingly "ruffled" by air currents, the lack of visible stars in the lunar sky, and aberrant shadows. This "proves" the astronauts were in a film studio, they argue, and the Moonscape was just a painted background. It was all faked.

Above: Film footage shows a chunk of Moon rock, said by sceptics to be a studio prop marked with a letter C. This photo was taken during the Apollo 16 mission in April 1972. The 'C' did not appear on the original film and may just be a coiled hair.

EVIDENCE
NAME

No visible stars are seen in Apollo photos because the landings took place during the bright lunar day, and Neil Armstrong's first step on lunar soil was filmed by a camera on the lander, not by a Hollywood film crew. Evidence from space suggests the truth.

Below: Apollo 17 astronaut Harrison Schmitt runs across the desolate surface of the Moon. This panoramic view was compiled from lunar photographs taken in 1972.

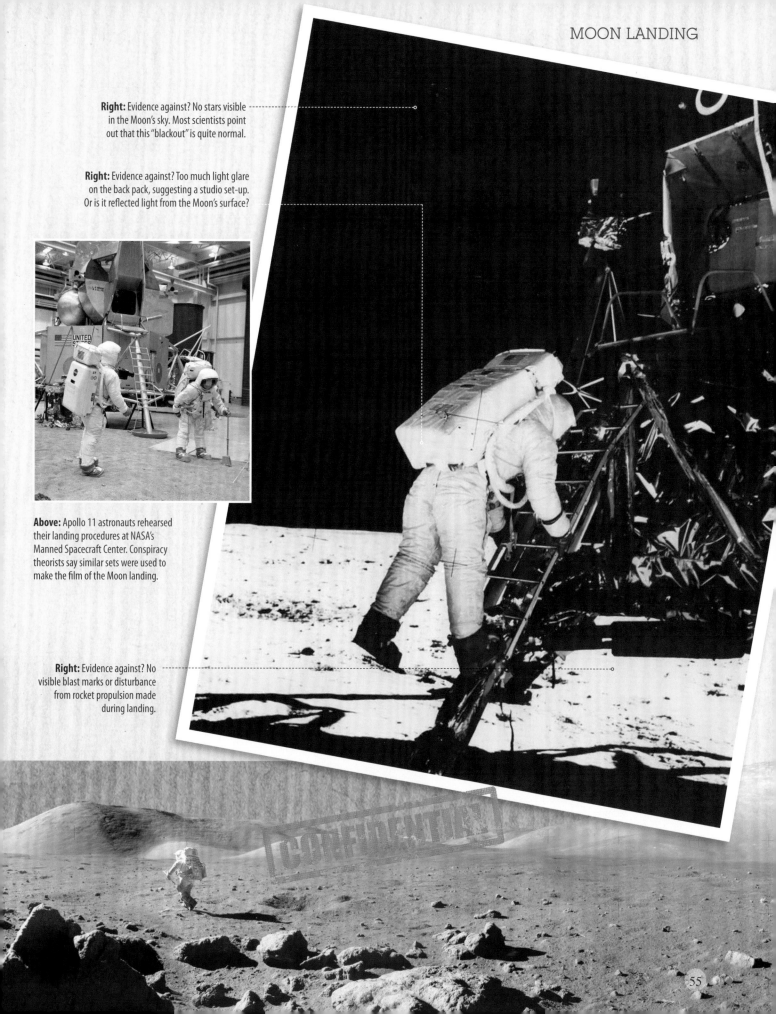

Right: Evidence against? No stars visible in the Moon's sky. Most scientists point out that this "blackout" is quite normal.

Right: Evidence against? Too much light glare on the back pack, suggesting a studio set-up. Or is it reflected light from the Moon's surface?

Above: Apollo 11 astronauts rehearsed their landing procedures at NASA's Manned Spacecraft Center. Conspiracy theorists say similar sets were used to make the film of the Moon landing.

Right: Evidence against? No visible blast marks or disturbance from rocket propulsion made during landing.

MARCH APRIL MAY JUNE **JULY 1969**

Above: A camera from *Surveyor 3*, a US robot craft that landed on the Moon in 1967, was returned to Earth by Apollo 12. There was evidence it had been on the Moon.

Above: Tests confirmed that Moon rock, brought back by Apollo 16, were the same age and origin as lunar meteorites found in Antarctica.

Could such a hoax be possible, even staged by film director Stanley Kubrick (of *2001* fame)? That Apollo 11 had reached the Moon was disputed by the Flat Earth Society, and by some Hindus, who said the Moon was much too far away. Propagandists in Russia and Cuba insisted that Soviet cosmonauts got to the Moon first. The "fake" claims presuppose that the astronauts lied, and that 40,000 or more NASA employees were in on the deception. Third-party evidence (not from NASA, the US government, or conspiracy theorists) includes photos taken by spacecraft, the existence of Moon rocks (382 kg/842 pounds) from six Apollo missions, and evidence that Apollo equipment is still on the Moon.

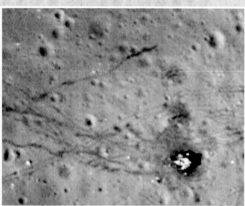

Above: This photograph, released by NASA in 2011, clearly shows the Apollo 17 Lunar Module on the surface of the Moon, wheel tracks left by the Lunar Rover and astronaut boot tracks. But could such a photo have been faked?

 THE TRUTH?

The most compelling evidence that the Apollo Moon landings did take place comes from recent fly-by observations of the landing sites by unmanned probes. Flying above the sites, the cameras revealed the presence of the landers and other equipment left by the Apollo crews. The Apollo landers appear to be on the Moon, to be checked out if and when future astronauts revisit— or are they?

Above: An astronomer at the Pic Du Midi Observatory in France made a telescope-sighting of Apollo 8 firing its engine during its 1968 round-the-Moon flight. Other observatories, such as Jodrell Bank in England, tracked the Apollo craft.

Left: The launch of Japan's lunar orbiter SELENE ("Kaguya") in 2007. Its photos of the Apollo 15 landing site showed dust-scatter from when the US craft left the Moon in 1971.

Right: Apollo 11's lunar laser ranging experiment package was left on the Moon. Signals reflected from it have been picked up on Earth.

PLANET X

There used to be nine planets in the Solar System, until Pluto was downgraded to dwarf planet status in 2006. But even before that, conspiracy theorists had postulated the existence of a mystery-planet, Planet X, hidden from us not just by limitless space but by deliberate deception.

One theory is that Planet X is the mysterious and legendary Nibiru. Proponents claim that Nibiru has featured in myths since ancient times. It is, they say, the origin of space-visitors who flew to Earth to genetically modify its inhabitants, and to shape the ancient civilizations of Egypt and Babylon.

According to one theory, Planet X is dangerously huge and following an orbital path that will send it close to Earth sometime in the not-too-distant future. The results of such a near-miss (let alone an impact—known as the "Nibiru cataclysm") could be catastrophic: earthquakes, floods, tsunamis, global warming, drought, and so on. To prevent mass panic, world governments—according to the conspiracists—have shut down on all information about Planet X. Many believers in the imminent approach of Planet X/Nibiru accuse NASA and other scientific bodies of deliberately covering up data gathered by space-telescopes, such as the Infrared Astronomical Satellite (IRAS), launched in 1983.

Left: Astronomer Percival Lowell (seen here in 1914) noted discrepancies in the orbits of Neptune and Uranus—possibly due to the gravitational pull of another planet. At first astronomers thought Pluto (spotted in 1930) was the unknown planet, but then they realized Pluto was too small.

 THE TRUTH?

Planet X is associated by some with the ending of the world, which was supposed to happen in 2012. It's strange that such a large object has remained invisible to the thousands of amateur astronomers with telescopes good enough to detect it.

Left: An artist's impression shows Planet X/Nibiru against the Earth's Moon. Some people associate Planet X with Trans-Neptunal Objects (TNOs), more than 1,000 bodies orbiting the Sun beyond the orbit of Neptune.

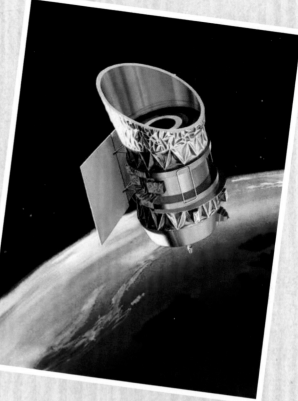

Above: The Infrared Astronomical Satellite (IRAS) scanned the solar system and far beyond. Planet X proponents claim astronomical data was concealed, to hide Planet X.

Left: It's alleged by conspiracists that the South Pole Telescope in Antarctica tracks and photographs Nibiru, which they say is visible only from the South Pole. Such claims cannot be upheld, however, as the SPT is a radio telescope, not an optical one, and it is not funded by either the US government or by NASA.

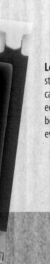

Left: V838 Mon is a distant star with what astronomers call an expanding light echo. This phenomenon has been taken as photographic evidence of Planet X.

26A

WAR STORIES

Silent conspiracies are as much a part of warfare as battles, and can be as deadly as the gun or bomb. Such has been the case ever since the Ancient Greeks tricked their way into Troy inside the wooden horse.

The first casualty of war is truth, as fact and fiction become confused. Historians argue over what really happened, while conspiracy theorists offer alternative readings of events— stories that make fascinating, if not always credible, reading. Did German scientists invent flying saucers as well as V-2 rockets? Did the US know of the Japanese plan to attack Pearl Harbor? Why were code-breaking secrets concealed for many years? World War II produced a cornucopia of controversy, none more so than in the last stages of the war in 1945, as the Allies tested the atomic bomb, and the Nazis in Hitler's Berlin bunker conspired how to evade their fate.

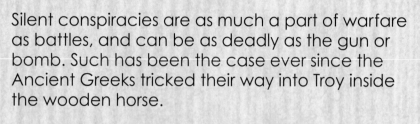

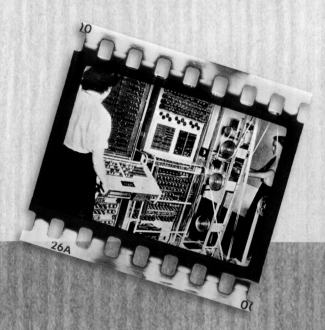

...N LADEN KILLED

A NATION CELEBRATES

...tice has been done

Seattle Times

...INNER OF EIGHT PULITZER PRIZES

2, 2011

seattletimes.com

THE NEWS TRIBU...

MONDAY · May 2, 2011

TNT · THENEWSTRIBUNE.COM

THE NEWSPAPER FOR THE SOU...

BIN LADEN SHOT
ENDING 10-YEAR H...

U.S. forces track him down in Pakistan, kill him

BY JULIE PACE
AND MATT APUZZO
The Associated Press

WASHINGTON - Osama bin Laden, the glowering mastermind behind the Sept. 11, 2001, terror attacks that killed thousands of Americans, was slain Sunday in a firefight with U.S. forces in Pakistan, ending a manhunt that spanned a frustrating decade.

"Justice has been done," President Barack Obama said in a dramatic late-night Sunday announcement at the White House.

ONLINE

Video of the celebration at the Freedom Bridge is available at www.thenewstribune.com.

INSIDE

South Sounders and state leaders react to Osama bin Laden's death. *See stories, back page*

A jubilant crowd of thousands gathered outside the White House as word spread of bin Laden's death. Hundreds more sang and waved American flags at Ground Zero in New York – where the twin towers that once stood as symbols of American economic power were brought down by bin Laden's hijackers 10 years ago. Another hi...

BARACK OBAMA

'His death does not mark the end.... We will remain vigilant.'

SPORTS **SCORES** INSIDE

THE NATION'S NEWSPAPER

USA TODAY

A GANNETT COMPANY

By Jeffrey M. Boan, AP
LeBron James: Drives past Celtics' Rajon Rondo.

Celtics feel the heat

Miami leads Eastern Conference semifinal with 99-90 win. NBA, 1, 10C

Jeff Bec...

Newsline

MONDAY, MAY 2, 2011

Osama bin Lad...
dead, Obama s...

...Pre...
killed him in a
targeted operation...

By Jim Michael...
USA...

A step toward s...

Masses of people fill ... Square to see John ... the former pope w...

NATO says it w...
Gadhafi; Rus...

Allied forces insist... destroying militar... about death of G...

Shuttle w...
Mother...

Rep. Gar... ...

As...

26A

0

26A

0

61

JUNE JULY AUGUST **SEPTEMBER 1944**

AUTHORIZED PERSONS ONLY

Above: A German V-2 rocket, seconds after launch in 1943. Allied intelligence got wind of the secret super-weapon, and knew there was no defence other than sabotage or bombing of rocket test sites and factories.

Below: A German radio operator of the Abwehr (Army intelligence). The German Army High Command ran reconnaissance (spying), signal-monitoring and counter-espionage operations.

SECRET WAR

World War II was a war of propaganda and secrets as much as military hardware. Secret agents crossed and double-crossed, and secret weapons were thought up and sketched on the backs of envelopes.

Britain had the better of things in the espionage war, with most German agents in the UK swiftly rounded up within months of the war starting in 1939. Some were jailed or executed, others "turned" into double-agents. It was never easy to tell who was who in the murky world of SIS and MI5, joined in 1940 by SOE, the Special Operations Executive, jokingly whispered of as "Churchill's Secret Army." Most spies were distinctly unglamorous—Arthur Owens, "a typical Welsh underfed type" according to his masters, ran a battery business, but was also agent SNOW working for the British and the Germans.

Backroom boffins devised all manner of weird ways in which to win the war. In 1944, as German rocket scientists were frantically trying to turn defeat into victory with new super-weapons such as the V-2 rocket and the bat-winged Horten jet fighter, German agents in France were being told to contaminate beer and wine, inject sausages with poison and prepare poisoned coffee, sugar, cigarettes and chocolate: the aim being to kill, disable and generally demoralize Allied soldiers and destabilize liberated areas.

NAME

📁 EVIDENCE

In 1944 Allied pilots reported seeing balls of fire zipping around aircraft. Could they be enemy secret weapons? Hallucinations? UFOs? The "foo fighters" as they were known (a term used to describe any unidentified flying objects at the time) became a wartime myth, for which scientists suggest natural phenomena such as St Elmo's Fire (ball lightning) as one explanation. A more fanciful explanation was that the Germans had invented a flying saucer with whizzing gas jets (the Fireball) to disrupt Allied bomber formations. However, German and Japanese pilots saw "foo fighters" too.

The Allies dreamed up counter-schemes of doubtful utility. One idea was to bomb Berlin not with propaganda leaflets or high explosives, but with poisonous snakes! Another notion was to hit German food production by poisoning German cows with cabbage leaves dosed with toxins. As preparations were made for the 1944 Normandy landings, the British "miscellaneous weapons" department came up with a new idea for breaching the Nazis' much-vaunted Atlantic Wall. The Panjandrum was a rocket-propelled two-wheeled cart, packed with explosive. It was supposed to trundle out of the sea from a landing craft, roll up the beach, blast through concrete and steel defences, and put the fear of God into the Germans. In trials, however, the Panjandrum showed an alarming tendency to run amok, spitting smoke and flames and sending its creators running in all directions. The eccentric project was quickly abandoned.

Top right: A rocket-propelled Panjandrum on the beach in Devon, England. Its "secret" tests were watched with incredulity by holidaymakers, but the exploding wheel never went into action.

Right: Careless Talk Costs Lives: one of the war's most famous propaganda lines. Bomber pilots were ordered never to discuss missions, even with family, in case security was compromised. As it was, crews seldom knew targets in advance.

"CHEERIO, OLD LAD, GOOD LUCK TOMORROW"

THEY TALKED...

...THIS HAPPENED

CARELESS TALK COSTS LIVES

MARCH APRIL MAY **JUNE 1944**

CODEBREAKERS AND D-DAY

The D-Day landings in 1944 marked the beginning of the end of World War II in Europe. Behind the vast armada lay a hidden army of code-breakers and planners.

Above: Two British naval Wrens adjust Colossus Mk II, the revolutionary programmable computer at Bletchley Park in England that greatly helped the success of D-Day. This computer had 2,500 vacuum tubes (valves).

Hardly anyone knew the secrets of a Victorian mansion estate 80 km (50 mi.) northwest of London. Bletchley Park, codenamed Station X, was home to a small army of code-breakers. Here almost every German secret signal was read and passed on by Station X's backroom geniuses, among them mathematicians Alan Turing and Max Newman, and Post Office engineer Tommy Flowers, who together helped create Colossus, the world's first programmable computer.

Helped by the Poles, who got hold of an Enigma cipher machine, the British had cracked Germany's military codes by 1940. The Germans had put too much faith in Enigma, and in the Lorenz cipher used by Hitler to communicate with his generals, but read by Station X, even though its code-breakers had never seen a Lorenz machine. The British shared their intelligence, codenamed Ultra, with the Americans.

Top left: Enigma was a 1918 banking design, modified in the 1930s by the German military so they could send coded messages. They put too much faith in its security.

Left: Bletchley Park, codename Station X, where the first codebreakers arrived under cover as a "shooting party" in September 1938.

Station X's code-breakers were crucial to the success of the Normandy landings on June 6, 1944. The Germans knew the invasion was coming, but not its location, and to mask the true battle plan Allied deception strategists did their utmost to confuse the enemy. They laid false trails everywhere, such as a nonexistent US army "based" in eastern England, with dummy airfields and dummy planes. Fake documents planted on a dead "British officer" (later known as "The Man Who Never Was") suggested to the Germans that Calais, not Normandy, was the Allies' target. Meanwhile "Monty's double," a Montgomery look-alike, toured bases in the Mediterranean to suggest to the Germans that the British commander was planning an attack in southern France.

Commandos were landed secretly on beaches in France to test out the sand and tides. Yet no deception could conjure an unopposed landing, so among the orthodox preparations for battle on the beaches were some "hush-hush" invasion-machines. These ingenious weapons, known as "Hobart's Funnies" (after Major General Percy Hobart) included "swimming" DD tanks (Shermans with propellers), Crab tanks armed with flails to detonate land mines, the Crocodile flame-thrower, and Bobbin tanks, which laid a canvas strip of roadway for transport following behind.

Above: America's Dwight D. Eisenhower, Supreme Commander of Allied forces in Europe (on the left) confers with Britain's Field Marshal Bernard Montgomery, commander of Allied ground forces during Operation Overlord, the Normandy invasion of 1944.

Below: Allied paratroops land on D-Day. To confuse the Germans, miniature dummy paratroops nicknamed "Ruperts" were also dropped from planes, complete with firecrackers to make them look more convincing.

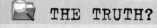

NAME

THE TRUTH?

Normandy was chosen as the D-Day target because the Germans did not expect an attack there—the region lacked ports for an invading army. So the Allies built two prefabricated harbors made from concrete and steel sections. Known as "Mulberries," they were towed by 150 tugs across the Channel. They served their purpose, although one was soon wrecked by fierce Channel storms.

Right: Admiral Husband E. Kimmel, commanding the US Pacific Fleet, bore the brunt of criticism for US military failings at Pearl Harbor. He was relieved of his command.

Below: Arthur H. McCollum's memorandum (7 October, 1940), from the Far East Asia section of US Naval Intelligence, proposed an 8-point plan to combat Japan. He suggested "If by any means Japan could be led to commit an overt act of war so much the better".

DECEMBER 1941

PEARL HARBOR

The Japanese attack on Pearl Harbor, on 7 December, 1941, brought the United States into World War II. Was it a surprise? Conspiracy theorists maintain that American (and British) intelligence knew of Japan's plan. The US administration allowed Pearl Harbor—to bring America into the war.

In 1941, the war in Europe was still going Germany's way. In Asia, Japan was winning in China, and was planning imperial expansion in the Pacific. US intelligence analyst Arthur H. McCollum suggested that only a direct attack on the US would sway a war-shy American public, even though Britain's prime minister, Winston Churchill, was desperate for US aid and was urging President Roosevelt to join the conflict. US Secretary of War Henry Stimson was expecting "impending hostilities", and so was shocked when the US Navy was caught unawares by the Japanese planes that roared in to devastate Pearl Harbor.

Did Churchill know what was coming, but keep quiet? Did secret telegrams from London warn of Japanese intentions? Some historians claim the British had cracked the JN-25 naval code, and knew of Japan's plans. The Americans did not pick up radio traffic, since the Japanese battle fleet used only flags and light signals. General "war warnings" were given to US forces, but nothing specific about Pearl. Why were the three US carriers out of port? Was it a ploy, to keep them out of danger? And if so, why leave eight battleships at anchor?

 THE TRUTH?

The US Navy believed Pearl Harbor was too shallow for a torpedo attack. Liaison between army and navy was poor, radar rudimentary and training leisurely. All three carriers were away, but USS Enterprise might have been hit had it returned on time.

7 OCTOBER 1940

ONI

OP-16-F-2

CONFIDENTIAL

MEMORANDUM FOR THE DIRECTOR

SUBJECT: ESTIMATE OF THE SITUATION IN THE PACIFIC AND RECOMMENDATIONS FOR ACTION BY THE UNITED STATES.

[memorandum body text]

NEWS

Sunday, December 7th, 1941 - Late Edition

WAR !! Japanese Bomb Pearl Harbor

Oahu hit in surprise attack - American fleet goes into action

Above: Across the United States, a shocked public read headline news of Pearl Harbor, a day most would never forget.

Right: Sailors in a launch rescue a man from the water as the battleship *USS West Virginia* burns following the Japanese attack. Eight US battleships were in Pearl Harbor.

Right: Posters demanding vengeance roused an angry American public, now ready for war not just in the Pacific but in Europe as well.

AVENGE December 7

Above: The interior of the *USS Arizona* war memorial at Pearl Harbor, commemorating the 2,388 people killed in the Japanese attack.

President Franklin D. Roosevelt

32 USA

Above: Pearl Harbor was the key that unlocked the might of America's war effort. Roosevelt called it "an unprovoked and dastardly attack".

67

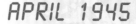

JANUARY FEBRUARY MARCH **APRIL 1945**

HITLER SUICIDE?

Above: Millions of victims of Nazi tyranny died in death camps such as Auschwitz-Birkenau. Hitler knew he could expect no mercy if captured.

Right: Adolf Hitler (in 1937). One bizarre theory claims Hitler had himself cloned. More credible is the suggestion that he had his lookalike "doppelganger", Gustav Weler, shot in an attempt to confuse the Allied troops, while he himself escaped from Berlin.

ESCAPE ROUTE
1 Berlin, Germany
2 Tonder, Denmark
3 Travemunde, Germany
4 Reus, Spain
5 Fuerteventura, Canary Isles
6 Mar Del Plata, Argentina

Did Adolf Hitler, the Nazi leader who had plunged the world into war, really die in April 1945 as the Soviet armies closed in? Did he kill himself, as the official histories claim? Or did Hitler escape and live on?

On April 28, 1945, as Soviet guns and tanks pounded Berlin, Adolf Hitler married Eva Braun in the Führer's underground bunker. The Nazi leader vowed he would not be taken prisoner. In the early hours of April 29, Hitler dictated for the last time to his secretary, Traudl Junge. Later, doubting the cyanide capsules he had been given, he ordered that they be tested on his dog, Blondi. To his distress, the dog died. On April 30, Hitler retired at 3:00 pm to his sitting room with Eva. At about 3:15 pm a shot was fired. Hitler's valet, Heinz Linge, testified he found Hitler dead, shot in the head. Hitler and Eva had also taken cyanide.

The bodies were wrapped in a rug, doused in petrol, and burned in a shell-crater. The survivors fled, to be killed, captured, or to disappear. On May 4, Soviet soldiers found charred remains of humans and two dogs, but Soviet leader Josef Stalin told American diplomats he believed Hitler had escaped.

Left: The suggested "escape route" to South America involved flight from Berlin, followed by an ocean-crossing in a U-boat. Two German U-boats arrived in Argentina in the summer of 1945.

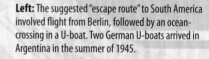

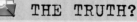 **THE TRUTH?**

Conspiracy theories suggest that Hitler faked his death and escaped to Argentina, where he lived with Eva until his death in 1962. Russian officials insist that a fragment of skull with a bullet hole in it, kept in the Russian State Archive, is proof of Hitler's suicide. However, American scientists disagree. After performing DNA tests on the skull in 2009, they claim it came from a woman aged under 40, not a man aged 56.

EXTRA THE STARS AND STRIPES **EXTRA**

HITLER DEAD

Fuehrer Fell at CP, German Radio Says; Doenitz at Helm, Vows War Will Continue

Churchill Hints Peace Is at Hand

Left and **above:** On May 2nd, 1945, Allied soldiers read news of Hitler's death in the US Army newspaper; the gun he used was reputedly a Walther PPK such as this one.

Top and above: The bomb-proof bunker in Berlin was where Hitler holed up as Soviet armies closed in. The map (inset) shows the Reich Chancellery layout, with the bunker in red.

Stories circulated of a secret tunnel, through which Hitler had fled. The official Soviet Communist line was that Hitler could have fled to Spain, Argentina, or even Japan. Later theories were wildly fantastic, suggesting, for example, that Hitler had escaped to a South Pole Nazi hideout that concealed an "inner world" (the Earth was hollow). The most bizarre theory was that Hitler flew, in a space rocket version of the V-2 missile, to a secret Moon base.

Top and above: Dr Josef Mengele, the Auschwitz "Angel of Death", fled to South America—as did Adolf Eichmann. Mengele was never caught, but Eichmann was found, tried and executed in Israel.

SEPTEMBER 2001

9/11

Above: 50,000 people worked in the World Trade Center, but not all were at work when, just before 8:46 am, United Airlines Flight 11 hit the North Tower. At 9:03 am United Airlines Flight 175 struck the South Tower, shown here in flames.

The 9/11 attacks on America in 2001 shocked the world and redirected US foreign policy to a "war on terror". Controversy shrouds that fateful day. Were there other conspirators besides the al-Qaeda suicide-bombers?

Four hijacked planes crashed on 9/11. Two hit the World Trade Center, a third hit the Pentagon. United Airlines Flight 93 crashed in Pennsylvania, after passengers fought with the hijackers. Nearly 3,000 people died. The official verdict was suicide terrorism, directed by al-Qaeda leader Osama bin Laden.

Conspiracy notions swirled among the rubble, and still circulate on the web. How had skyscrapers fallen so quickly, unless blown up by demolition charges? How could hijackers fly a plane straight into the tightly-guarded Pentagon? Why were the airliners not shot down? Did President Bush know before he was told the news at a school in Sarasota, Florida? Alternative "suspects" in the web of 9/11 fantasy were: right-wing US groups; Israel; China; the World Trade Center's owners; the CIA in collaboration with al-Qaeda, possibly using missiles hologrammed to look like airliners; the covert New World Order; evil "Thetans" (invisible powers according to Scientologists); and gold thieves seeking bullion kept in the World Trade Center.

Above: Rescuers help victims at the Pentagon, hit at 9:37 am by American Airlines Flight 77. Witnesses reported seeing an airliner fly into the building.

Right: This map shows the flight paths across the eastern USA of the four hijacked planes: two from Boston (11 and 175), one from New Jersey (93), and one from Washington (77).

NAME

THE TRUTH?

Many people saw the Twin Towers struck on live TV. Flight 77's recorders and DNA from victims indicated airliner impact. On October 7, the US and allies attacked Afghanistan. All 19 hijackers were dead, but their accomplices were rigorously pursued. Osama bin Laden was killed by US forces in 2011.

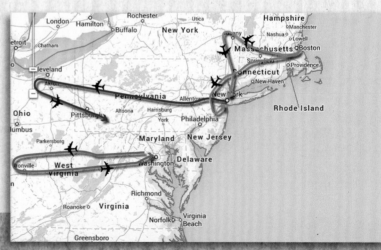

Below: Firefighters and media stand at Ground Zero, in the rubble of the World Trade Center. At 9:59 am, the South Tower collapsed, followed 29 minutes later by the North Tower. At 5:21 pm the smaller building, known as 7 World Trade Center, also fell.

THE
9/11
COMMISSION
REPORT
FINAL REPORT OF THE NATIONAL COMMISSION ON
TERRORIST ATTACKS UPON THE UNITED STATES

Left: 9/11 conspiracy supporters demonstrated in Denver, Colorado, in August 2008. Conspiracy theories threw suspicion on the CIA and military. Did Wall Street have foreknowledge? Had the government staged 9/11 to justify US wars in Afghanistan and Iraq?

Above: The 9/11 Commission report concluded that the planes' impact fatally damaged the Twin Towers, spewing burning fuel over many floors and causing total collapse. There were no missiles, no hidden explosives, and no conspiracy other than Al-Qaeda's.

SPIES, LIES AND SCANDAL

Nothing excites conspiracy theorists more than the whiff of scandal in high places, stories denied by official sources, and lurid tales of double agents and triple-crosses.

During the Cold War years of the 1940s to 1980s, conspiracies and fears of conspiracies proliferated. Even in the pre-web age, everything believable was credible, everything incredible equally believable. Who was telling the truth? Before the Internet, what went on behind closed doors was known only to a few, though whispered by millions. Scandal reached to the corridors of power, into bedrooms and boardrooms, and conspiracies mushroomed in the murky world of espionage. It snared celebrities, and entranced a public ever more fascinated by a James Bond world of spies, moles, sex secrets, mystery deaths, disappearances, cover-ups and dirty deeds behind closed doors.

MARCH APRIL MAY JUNE

1940s-1960s

THE CAMBRIDGE SPIES

In the 1950s Britain's security services were made to look leaky. The Cambridge spies were revealed, only for three of them to escape across the Iron Curtain.

With the Cold War at its height, spies were all the rage in fiction. In reality too, "moles" and "sleepers" were deeply embedded in Britain's intelligence community. Most notorious were the "Cambridge spies," a group "converted" to communism and recruited as Soviet agents while students at Cambridge University in the 1930s. The four were Kim Philby, Guy Burgess, Donald Maclean and Anthony Blunt.

Of the four, the master spy was Philby. He joined MI6 in 1940 and later worked at the British embassy in Washington, acting as link between British intelligence and the Americans, while passing on secrets to the Russians at the height of the Cold War. Burgess and Maclean worked at the Foreign Office in London, also spying for the Russians. They got away with it until 1951, when both men disappeared, turning up publicly in Moscow in 1956. They had fled Britain after being tipped off by Philby, with whom Burgess had worked in Washington, that their cover as moles and spies was about to be blown. Philby maintained his cover, even after he was "named" as a double agent by a Labour MP in 1955, when he was "cleared" by the Foreign Office. However, he was shifted out of the diplomatic service, and was working in the Lebanon as a journalist when, in 1963, he defected to the Soviet Union by sea, apparently fearing he was about to be abducted.

The Fourth Man was Sir Anthony Blunt, art expert and curator of the Queen's paintings. Blunt privately admitted to being a spy in 1964 in return for immunity from prosecution, but he was finally publicly unmasked in 1979, and stripped of his knighthood.

How many secrets, and how many Western agents, were betrayed by the Cambridge spies is probably beyond estimation.

Above: The headquarters of the Russian secret service in Moscow. During the Cold War, the KGB ran agents in many Western countries, and between 1954 and 1991 was all-powerful.

Below: Within the fairytale-looking Kremlin, the old Soviet leadership fought the Cold War—and conspired against one another.

Москва-Кремль - Moscou-Kremlin Общий Вид - Vue générale.

THE TRUTH?

NAME

Speculation persisted about a "Fifth Man." There were probably more than five Cambridge spies. Blunt (the "talent-spotter") and Burgess were members of the Apostles, an exclusive university society. Another Apostle was John Cairncross, named as a Soviet spy in 1990. Some have cast doubt on the double role of Sir Roger Hollis, MI5 boss from 1956 to 1965.

Above: Kim Philby, most notorious of the so-called Cambridge spies, strolls around Moscow in 1968 after his defection.

Right: Anthony Blunt had enjoyed a certain eminence as art adviser to the Queen, while secretly passing information to the Russians, a mission he had begun in the 1930s as a Cambridge recruiter of spies.

Above: British Labour leader Hugh Gaitskell addressing his party Conference in Brighton in October 1962. He died in January 1963, and was replaced by Harold Wilson, a long-time rival. Wilson was Britain's prime minister by the following year.

JANUARY 1963

MOLES AND MURDERS

British Prime Minister Harold Wilson believed he was a target for the intelligence services. And was tycoon Robert Maxwell murdered by Israeli secret agents?

By the 1950s, most left-leaning politicians were anxious to shy away from any youthful flings with communism, in the hard light of Stalinist tyranny and Iron Curtain repression that had tarnished the socialist Utopian ideal. In the United States, McCarthyism had led to a vilification and witch-hunts for "Reds under the bed."

Could it be that Labour leader Harold Wilson, Oxford don and Huddersfield Town football fan, was a Soviet mole? Soviet defector and ex-KGB man Anatoliy Golitsyn said he was, after hearing gossip in KGB corridors about secret poisons. According to Golitsyn, the KGB wanted to remove Hugh Gaitskell as Labour leader and install "their man" Wilson. Gaitskell died suddenly in 1963: the conspiracy version is that his fatal illness came after drinking poisoned coffee at the Soviet Embassy. Wilson succeeded him, becoming Britain's prime minister in 1964. In his second term of office (1974–1976), Wilson apparently thought the British intelligence services were plotting against him, believed the lavatory in 10 Downing Street was bugged, and told future president George H. W. Bush (then head of the CIA) that he was being spied on. Wilson's resignation in 1976 came as a surprise, though prime ministers Callaghan and Thatcher found no evidence of any plot against him "by or within the security service."

Left: Harold Wilson in 1964. The Wilson government remained an ally of the United States, but refused to commit troops to the Vietnam War.

NAME

THE TRUTH?

James J. Angleton, a key figure in CIA counter-intelligence from 1954 to 1975, was privately convinced that several Western leaders were sympathetic to, if not actively working for, Moscow. He named Canada's prime minister Pierre Trudeau, Sweden's Olof Palme, West Germany's Willy Brandt—and Harold Wilson.

A prominent figure in the Wilson years and later was publishing boss Robert Maxwell. Born Jan Hoch in Czechoslovakia, Maxwell (it was alleged) became a Soviet agent during World War II, at the same time as he was winning medals in the British Army. In his post-war publishing career, Maxwell did many deals across the Iron Curtain, and prospered. It has also been alleged that he was at the same time working for the Israeli secret service, Mossad. The story is that by 1990, with his empire in financial meltdown, Maxwell was asked by the KGB to help remove Russian reformer Mikhail Gorbachev in return for cash. He was supposed to bring the Israelis (and through them the Americans) on board, but the Israelis refused. Maxwell demanded a pay-off to solve his business problems and keep quiet, and was eliminated as a dangerous liability.

Below and top right: Robert Maxwell, seldom out of the news, owned Mirror Group Newspapers at the time he gave this press conference in April 1991. His businesses were in trouble, and his death later that year aroused much speculation. The tycoon's body was found in the sea, supposedly after he died while alone on the deck of his yacht, the Lady Ghislaine.

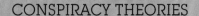

Below: Georgi Markov in 1978. The Bulgarian dissident's murder was carried out by an assassin wielding a lethal umbrella.

Bottom: Markov worked for the BBC World Service in London, and was waiting at a city bus stop when his assailant struck.

SEPTEMBER 1978

LICENSED TO KILL

Although, as far as we know, 007-style intrigue is not that common in the real world of espionage and counter-intelligence, mysterious deaths do sometimes happen.

In September 1978, Bulgarian writer and anti-communist dissident Georgi Markov died in a London hospital. Three days earlier he had felt unwell at his desk at the BBC World Service, complaining of a "sting" on his thigh. He had, it transpired, been the victim of a hit by Bulgarian secret agents. On September 8, Markov had been waiting at a bus stop when he felt something jab the back of his leg. Looking round, he saw a man picking up an umbrella. The man jumped into a cab. Markov became ill, but treatment in hospital failed to save him and he died three days later. An autopsy revealed that he had been "shot" with a tiny pellet containing toxic ricin, which had been absorbed into his bloodstream. There was no antidote to ricin poisoning.

Umbrella handle

Trigger in handle

Linkage connecting trigger to valve

Cylinder of compressed air

Switch that activates valve

Valve that fires ricin pellet

Right: The Markov murder-umbrella had a trigger in the handle to release a compressed-air valve mechanism. This injected a fatal pellet of ricin into the victim, who felt little more than a sting.

78

A similarly mysterious but more public death came in 2006. Alexander Litvinenko was a former KGB agent, who had sought political asylum in Britain. He accused the Russian Federal Protective Service (FPS) of terrorist atrocities as part of its plan to destabilize the "new Russia" and insert Vladimir Putin as leader. Litvinenko had put himself in the line of fire. On November 1, 2006, he was taken ill with a mysterious radiation sickness, and died three weeks later in hospital.

Litvinenko had been poisoned with radioactive polonium-210, possibly at a sushi restaurant, or in a cup of tea he drank at a London hotel. Russian agent Andrei Lugovoi was charged with murder in May 2007, provoking a furious diplomatic row between Britain and Russia, but by then he was back home out of reach. Later, a second Russian agent, Dmitri Kovtun, was also implicated. Neither is likely ever to be extradited to face trial. Lugovoi prospered, becoming a member of the Russian parliament, but Kovtun remained less prominent.

NAME

THE TRUTH?

Radiation poison leaves a trail. Litvinenko's assassins contaminated themselves with polonium travelling from Germany to London. Traces were found on a couch in a room where Kovtun spent the night, in his car, and at a restaurant. Litvinenko's deathbed accusation that Russian intelligence and Vladimir Putin had conspired to kill him led to worldwide media coverage. Unofficially, the British authorities believed "we are 100% sure who administered the poison, where and how," but Andrei Lugovoi and Dmitri Kovtun were by then thousands of miles away.

Above: Andrei Lugovoi, suspected of involvement in the killing of Alexander Litvinenko in 2006, at a press conference in Moscow in 2007. Both had links to the KGB.

Right: Litvinenko's London home was examined by police forensic and scene of crime officers as they attempted to follow the trail of radioactive poison back to his killers.

MARCH APRIL MAY JUNE JULY 1961

FILE

SEX IN HIGH PLACES

The Profumo affair had sex, lies and spies, all in one heady cocktail. A government minister became the center of a scandal involving prostitutes, parties and nuclear secrets.

The story began in 1960 when 18-year-old Christine Keeler got a job in a Soho club. After meeting Stephen Ward, an osteopath with connections, Keeler and her blonde friend Mandy Rice-Davies became on-call party girls. In July 1961, at a party at Cliveden, the Astors' estate, Keeler cavorting nude in the swimming pool, caught the eye of War Minister John Profumo. High profile and married to actress Valerie Hobson, Profumo embarked on a fling with Keeler.

Keeler was generous with her favors. At the same time as she was going to bed with Profumo, she was seeing Yevgeni (Eugene) Ivanov, Soviet naval attaché and spy. It's unlikely that Profumo chatted in bed about military secrets with Keeler, a girl more interested in a good time than in nuclear payloads, but after MI5 got wind and issued a quiet warning, Profumo quickly ended the affair. By now whispers were circulating about "a minister and a call-girl."

Above: Mandy Rice Davies, the blonde in the Keeler-Profumo affair. Her remark made in court "Well he would, wouldn't he?" (in response to a witness denying he'd ever met her) passed into journalistic folklore.

Below right: Christine Keeler, the center of media attention outside London's Marylebone magistrates' court in 1963 during the trial that rocked the Macmillan government.

NAME

 EVIDENCE?

Stephen Ward's death while on trial was ruled to be suicide. But some people speculated at the time that the security services had "eliminated" him, to prevent more revelations about sex parties and prominent people. Ivanov went back to Moscow, his wife left him, and he died in 1994. John Profumo redeemed his reputation by years of charity work, his wife Valerie Hobson stuck by him, and Profumo died in 2006.

In 1962, Keeler's lover Aloysius "Lucky" Gordon stabbed another of her lovers, Johnny Edgecombe. The case of the good-time girl with drug-dealer boyfriends led to open press interest and rumors about her involvement with a government minister. In March 1963, after allegations voiced in the House of Commons (protected by MPs' privilege), Profumo denied any impropriety. But the cat was now out of the bag, and in June, the War Minister resigned, admitting that he had lied about his relationship with Keeler.

MI5 interviewed Christine Keeler and, while judging her no Mata Hari, decided there was at least a chance that Ivanov, using Stephen Ward as a go-between, could have used Keeler as a "honey-trap" to wheedle secrets from Profumo. Ward was arrested and charged with living on money from prostitution; in August he was found dead at home, from an overdose of sleeping pills. The report on the Profumo affair came out in September and in October Prime Minister Harold Macmillan resigned, on health grounds. Keeler was jailed for nine months for perjury, while the Conservative government staggered on into 1964, when Labour easily won the general election.

Top: Monica Lewinsky in 1999. President Clinton's "was it sex or wasn't it?" liaison with the young intern earned her fleeting notoriety. This is another example of a scandalous affair in office.

Above: Postage stamp from the Comoros Islands, showing a beaming US President Bill Clinton, First Lady Hillary Clinton—and Monica Lewinsky!

Left: Cliveden, home of the Astors from 1893. It was here that John Profumo saw Christine Keeler at a pool party that became notorious.

APRIL MAY JUNE JULY **AUGUST 1997**

DEATH OF DIANA

Diana, Princess of Wales, died on August 31, 1997, in a car crash in Paris. Her death became a *cause célèbre*. Was it an accident, or the result of a high-level conspiracy, as many of Diana's devotees wanted to believe?

The official cause of the accident was high speed, and heavy drinking by the driver, Henri Paul. Sceptics claimed Paul was not drunk; he was either framed or was working for MI6. The involvement of the British secret service was alleged by former MI6 agent Richard Tomlinson, who claimed Diana was bugged and followed. Had a white Fiat Uno, never traced, collided with the Mercedes? This seems an unlikely method for murder. Did spooks flash lights into the driver's eyes? Absurd, according to experts. The victims, Diana and her boyfriend Dodi Fayed, were not wearing seat belts. Had their belts been tampered with? In 2006, a police inquiry (Operation Paget) was opened into the conspiracies surrounding Diana's death. It found that any surveillance had been routine.

Below: The crashed Mercedes in the Pont d'Alma tunnel. The first emergency call was timed at 12:26 am, but Diana did not reach hospital until 2:06; she went into cardiac arrest and was treated in the ambulance, but was beyond help.

Below: The entrance to the road tunnel into which the Mercedes car accelerated at high speed, pursued by photographers.

Below: Diana was an international media target, a victim of the celebrity she had often welcomed after her marriage breakup.

AT A GLANCE

Diana and Dodi Fayed left the Ritz Hotel at 12.20 am. Driver Henri Paul drove off at over twice the speed limit, to elude photographers. At 12.23 the car crashed. Fayed and Paul were killed outright. Diana died later in hospital. Security man Trevor Rees-Jones survived, but was badly injured.

At the inquest, details emerged of a letter that Diana had written to her butler: "this part of my life is the most dangerous", she wrote. She went on to say that her husband, Prince Charles, was planning "an accident" in her car, so that he could remarry. A close friend of Diana, Lucia Flecha de Lima, dismissed the letter as a possible forgery. Operation Paget found no evidence of a conspiracy, and concluded that Diana's death was the result of a tragic accident.

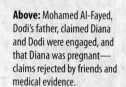

Above: Mohamed Al-Fayed, Dodi's father, claimed Diana and Dodi were engaged, and that Diana was pregnant—claims rejected by friends and medical evidence.

Above: Prince Philip, Charles' father and Diana's ex-father-in-law. The inquest dismissed suggestions that he or any member of the British royal family was involved in Diana's death.

Below: The Imperial Suite at the Ritz, Paris. Here Diana and Dodi Fayed ate dinner before the fateful dash from the hotel.

Above: This is the route through central Paris taken by the Mercedes and the pursuing paparazzi.

LAB LEGENDS

Scientists have done much to make human life better—we enjoy improved health, for example, thanks to medical advances. We also exchange news instantly, across continents—thanks to modern communications and information technology.

However, scientific advances are not always innocent and harmless. Conspiracy theorists worry less about Frankenstein lab monsters, and more about the frightening, covert use of mind-control and behavior-modification with drugs and seriously nasty psychiatric methods. Under the guise of progress and "health benefits", science and commerce together have changed how people live, all over the world. We consume food additives, for example, without thinking about it. Discouraging us from smoking is reasonable enough for most people, but we would all like to be certain that the air we breathe is pure, the water we drink is harmless, and that no-one is trying to be Big Brother and tell us how to think.

MARCH APRIL MAY JUNE 1953

MK-ULTRA MIND CONTROL

How better to win a war than to gain control of the minds of the enemy? That was the aim of the secret MK-Ultra human research program into behavior modification, run by the CIA's Scientific Intelligence Division in the 1950s and 60s.

The project came about partly as a response to communist claims during the Korean War that US prisoners of war in North Korea had been "brainwashed" into expressing sympathy for communism. It was also born of the CIA's growing frustration at not being able to penetrate the Iron Curtain with agents, and from fear of communist enemies within. The MK-Ultra project was headed by CIA chemist Sidney Gottlieb, known as the "Black Sorcerer" for his skill in preparing lethal poisons. Under Gottlieb's direction, the MK-Ultra team sought to develop mind-control drugs to counter communist brainwashing. They also wanted to be able to program individuals to carry secrets of which they were unaware—until "woken". Trial participants were unwittingly subjected to drugs such as LSD, as well as hypnosis, sensory deprivation, torture, sexual and verbal abuse, and enforced isolation.

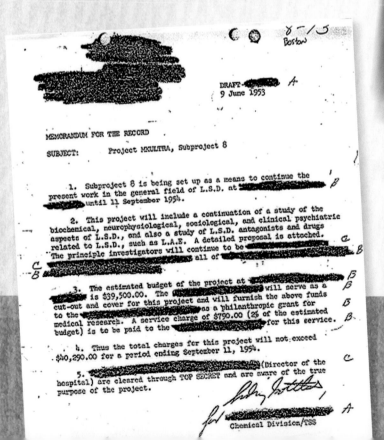

Left: In June 1953, Dr Sidney Gottlieb wrote this letter approving the use of LSD for mind-control experiments.

Left: Bio-warfare scientist Frank Olson died in 1953 after falling from a ninth-floor window of the Hotel Pennsylvania, New York. Was it drug-induced suicide, or a CIA elimination after Olson took part in MK-Ultra trials and became seriously disturbed?

Above: 1960s drug culture popularized "magic mushrooms", from which psilocybin was synthesized by Swiss scientist Albert Hoffman. He also first extracted LSD (seen here on a sugar lump) from ergot rye fungus. Both drugs are hallucinogenic.

Above: Conspiracy theorists believe LSD was secretly tested on prostitutes and drug addicts, who were picked up from bars in San Francisco and taken to safehouses. This was part of the CIA plan to create a drug-culture "weapon".

Right: A memorandum from 1953 lists experiments, such as "hypnotically induced anxieties", from the MK-Ultra program.

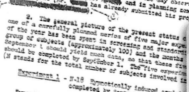

DRAFT-SO/111
11 May 1953

MEMORANDUM FOR THE RECORD

SUBJECT: Visit to Project

THE TRUTH?

Precursors to MK-Ultra were Projects Artichoke and Bluebird. These evolved from Operation Paperclip in 1945, the Allied program to recruit Nazi scientists after Germany's defeat in World War II. As the Cold War froze harder in the 1950s, the US intelligence community feared communist use of mind-control for subversion and espionage, and embarked on MK-Ultra as a counter-measure.

MARCH APRIL MAY JUNE 1953

Right: The drug mescaline was linked to the death in 1953 of tennis player Harold Blauer. He allegedly died after drug tests run by the US Office of Scientific Intelligence (part of the CIA).

Above: Molecular model of the drug BZ; this hallucinogen is possibly still being tested on soldiers, with reports of people suffering alarming "incapacitating" effects after being given it.

MK-Ultra's extreme methods were used on individuals to promote dependence, illogical and impulsive thinking, cause amnesia and mental confusion, and to make sure a person would not "confess" under interrogation. The research was undertaken at colleges and universities, hospitals, prisons and pharmaceutical companies, sometimes knowingly, at other times through CIA "front organizations".

In 1973, with the Watergate scandal unfolding and the unpopularity of the Vietnam War to the fore, CIA director Richard Helms ordered the destruction of all MK-Ultra files in an attempt to conceal any evidence of the CIA's questionable, if not outright illegal, activities. Nevertheless, the project was brought to public attention by the Church Committee of the US Congress in 1975. Then, in 1977, the Freedom of Information Act brought more information to light, and in 2001 some facts about the project were declassified.

Above: Richard M. Helms was US Director of Central Intelligence from 1966 to 1973, the year he ordered MK-Ultra documents to be destroyed.

Above: US Senator Frank Church headed the 1975 Committee that brought the whole MK-Ultra issue to public attention.

Above: Scottish-born D. Ewen Cameron, a psychiatrist on the MK-Ultra program, is alleged to have used electric-therapy and LSD in human trials, with shocking effects.

NAME

AT A GLANCE

Conspiracy theorists allege that MK-Ultra still goes on, with more advanced techniques now used to program agents, even for assassinations. There are also suggestions that shadowy forces "run" media stars and politicians, too. MK-Ultra has an ongoing influence, even if the program is officially over.

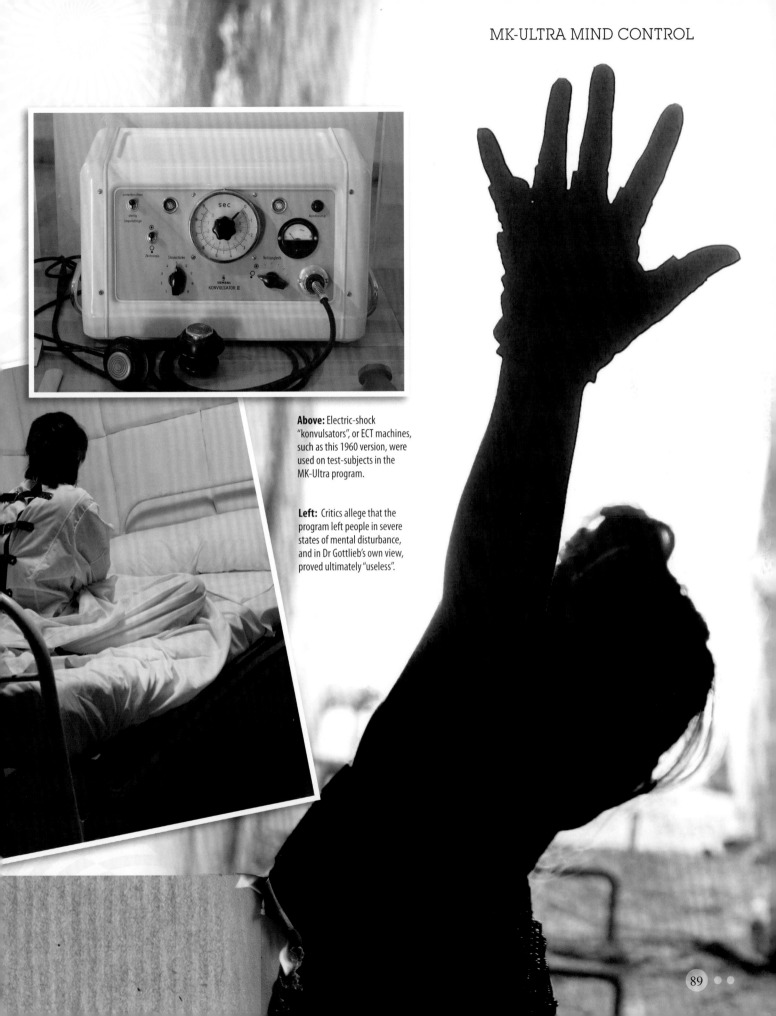

Above: Electric-shock "konvulsators", or ECT machines, such as this 1960 version, were used on test-subjects in the MK-Ultra program.

Left: Critics allege that the program left people in severe states of mental disturbance, and in Dr Gottlieb's own view, proved ultimately "useless".

FLUORIDE IN WATER

Is adding fluoride to water a safe way to ensure gleaming white, cavity-free smiles? In 1969 the World Health Organization endorsed fluoridation. But was fluoride a dental breakthrough, or a sinister side-effect of the atomic age infringing rights and threatening health?

Fluorides are compounds containing fluorine (chemical symbol F). In the 1930s, scientists discovered that fluoride reduces tooth decay. By the 1950s, many Americans were drinking fluoridated water and using fluoride toothpaste.

Critics cited harmful side-effects of fluoride, both to teeth and health in general. On ethical grounds they argued that fluoridation violated the Human Rights Act and the UN Convention on the Rights of the Child. Supporters retorted that fluoride posed minimal health risks, in return for fewer fillings. A healthy fluoride level in water of 1 part per million was considered "safe".

Left: Beware the red in the tube. This 1953 flier linked public health campaigns with communist/intrusive state threats to an uninformed public.

Right: Fit to drink? Since the 1950s people have trusted water companies to supply clean water. This involves chemical treatment, but how much is ethical?

NAME

THE TRUTH?

In England, about 10% of people drink fluoridated water: in the US the figure is about 60%. Canada, Australia, New Zealand and Ireland all fluoridate water. Europe is less keen: Germany, France, Belgium and Switzerland all do not. Countries that don't fluoridate water also report falls in dental decay: possibly because of fluoride toothpaste, improving oral hygiene and diet.

Conspiracy theorists take the view that fluoridation was part of a plan to control the American people. In 1945, US scientist Charles Perkins was told by a German fluoride manufacturer that the Germans had added fluoride to water to keep prisoners docile. Did government agencies take note? Recently declassified documents have revealed that vast quantities of toxic fluoride were needed to make the first atomic bombs, and fluoride became a major health hazard to people working for the bomb program. It's alleged that "Program F" was a US cover-up. Evidence of fluoride's dangers were suppressed, and instead fluoride was promoted as a dental marvel. The debate continues.

unknown
80-100%
60-80%
40-60%
20-40%
1-20%
<1%

Left: This map of the world shows the extent of fluoridated water usage. Colors indicate the percentage of population in each country that receives fluoridated water.

Left: An anti-fluoride protest was held in San Francisco in 2013. The "fluoride prevents tooth decay" myth is, sceptics claim, a smokescreen to hide health fears, even its use as a mind-control agent.

Above: The first atomic-bomb test, July 1945. Fluoride use in the top-secret Manhattan A-bomb project is said to have caused environmental and health damage. Was the "fluoride is good for teeth" campaign a cover-up, and Cold War paranoia an excuse to bury bad news?

HOAXES

The purpose of a hoax is to delude the public, either to protect a vested interest or simply to make someone a profit. Conspiracy theorists will often argue that what science dismisses as a hoax is in fact the truth.

Some hoaxes, such as the famous case of Piltdown Man (a prehistoric fossil that wasn't), amuse us. Others, such as the mystery of the Turin Shroud, may cause us to wonder. Despite our shrinking world and expanding scientific knowledge, there still seems to be room for belief in unknown creatures—such as the Yeti, Bigfoot and the Loch Ness Monster—that keep academic establishments guessing. The story of "the one that got away" is often the most entertaining, but most people were grateful that the Millennium Bug, at the turn of the century, was one conspiracy bug that failed to bite.

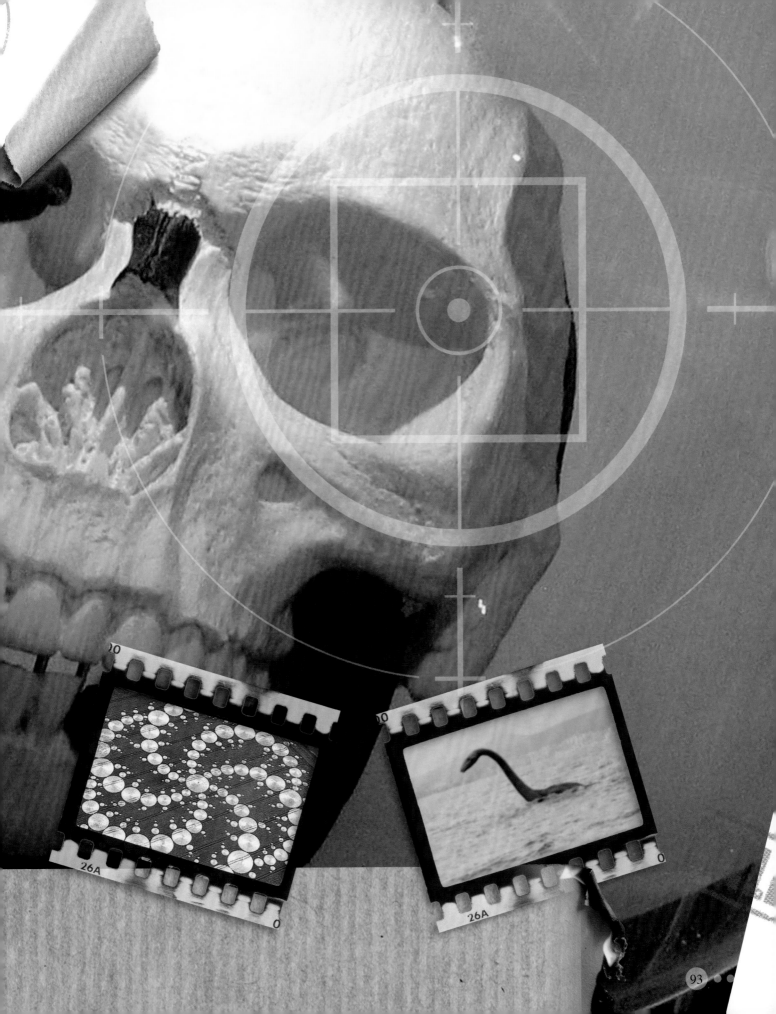

NOVEMBER 1974

LORD ON THE RUN

The "Case of the Vanishing Peer" hit the headlines in 1974. Did Lord Lucan conspire with a hit-man to have his wife murdered, only for things to go horribly wrong? Or did he get away with murder himself?

Richard John Bingham, 7th Earl of Lucan (born 1934) was Establishment Man: Eton, Coldstream Guards, City banker, wife and three children, house in Belgravia, lucky at cards. By 1974, however, "Lucky" Lucan had run out of luck. He had money problems, and he and his wife were estranged and battling over their three children. He told friends Lady Lucan was going mad.

Between 8:30 and 9:00 pm on Thursday November 7, 1974, the Lucans' nanny Sandra Rivett, having put the two younger children to bed, went down to make a pot of tea. Upstairs at 46 Lower Belgrave Street, Lady Lucan was watching TV. Lord Lucan was at his flat or his club. Downstairs, Sandra Rivett was battered to death. At 9:15 pm, Lady Lucan went to see what had happened to the tea, whereupon (she told police) she was attacked by her husband, but fought him off. With blood on his clothes, Lucan confessed to killing Sandra by mistake. At 9:45 pm, Lady Lucan, injured and bloodstained, fled to the Plumber's Arms. The police discovered the body and a length of lead pipe, but Lucan had gone.

Lucan's story was that he had disturbed an intruder assaulting his wife, but fearing she would accuse him, he had fled. His friends reckoned that he had drowned himself by scuttling his boat in the English Channel, remorseful that he had killed the wrong woman. Another theory was that Lucan had hired a hit-man to kill his wife, and that when he found the wrong body in the sack, Lucan then attacked his wife himself. At the inquest, Lucan was named as the murderer. In 1999, the High Court declared the vanishing peer officially "deceased." Unconfirmed sightings of Lucan, however, continue to this day.

Above: Lady Lucan with photo albums recalling the early, happier days of her marriage to Lucan. Whether she was the intended murder victim will never be known.

NAME
THE TRUTH?

Rumors persisted that friends had smuggled Lucan out of the country to begin a new life in Africa. Then, in a 2012 TV documentary, a personal assistant of Lucan's close friend John Aspinall said that on Aspinall's instructions, she had arranged for Lucan's two eldest children to visit Africa between 1979 and 1981, so that their father could see how they were growing up without making contact with them. Lady Lucan denied that the children had been to Africa at that time.

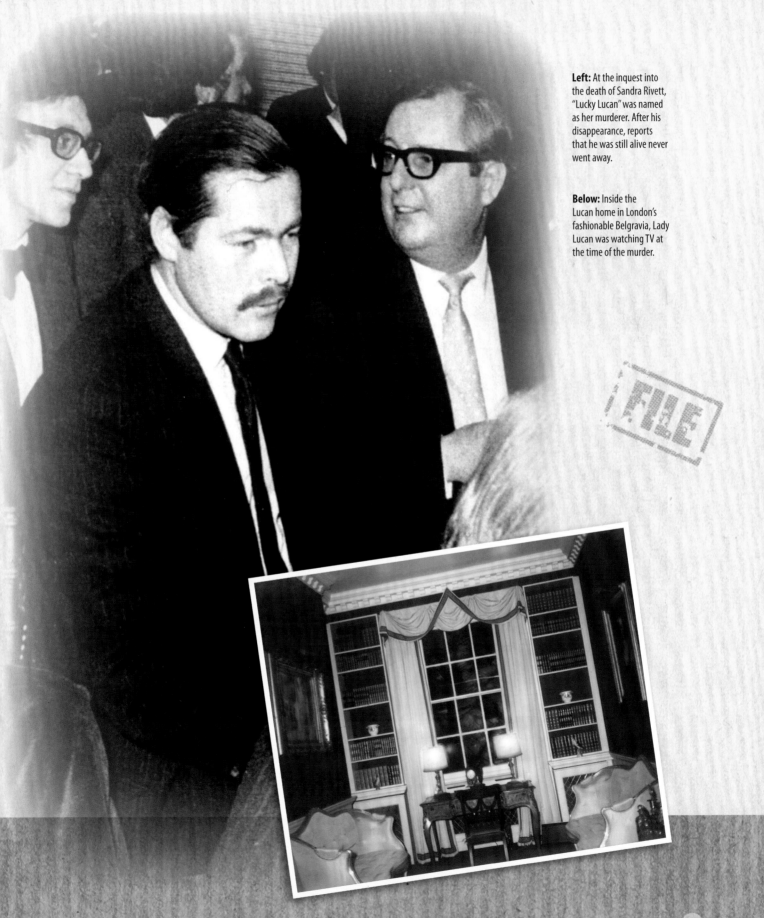

Left: At the inquest into the death of Sandra Rivett, "Lucky Lucan" was named as her murderer. After his disappearance, reports that he was still alive never went away.

Below: Inside the Lucan home in London's fashionable Belgravia, Lady Lucan was watching TV at the time of the murder.

PILTDOWN MAN

Piltdown Man is one of the most famous hoaxes in palaeontology. For some 40 years, it fooled the scientific establishment, who thought that a "missing link" in human evolution had been discovered.

Piltdown Man wasn't in fact a whole man, merely fragments of a skull and jawbone. In December 1912, newspaper headlines revealing the 1908 discovery in a gravel pit in southern England caused a sensation.

For centuries the fossil evidence for prehistoric life had puzzled people. Fossils dug up by farmers were explained away as the remains of dragons, giants or animals drowned in Noah's Flood. In the early 1800s, finds of extinct giant reptiles led to an outbreak of "dinosaur fever," but exactly how humans had evolved remained a mystery.

Then, in 1912, what appeared to be a prehistoric "skull" was discovered in Sussex. The *Manchester Guardian* newspaper called the find "by far the earliest trace of mankind that has yet been found in England." Piltdown man, named after a village in Sussex, seemed to be the "missing link" between apes and humans.

The find was credited to local solicitor and fossil-hunter Charles Dawson, and named *eoanthropus dawsoni*. Dawson claimed more finds: a tooth in 1913, and another tooth and more bones in 1915. He died in 1916, but Piltdown Man's place in history seemed secure. In 1950, a reconstruction of a head was made based on the bones. Then, in 1953, just as Britain was celebrating the conquest of Everest and the coronation of Elizabeth II, "Piltdown Man" was declared a fake. People questioned how such a hoax could have escaped detection without the compliance of an expert.

Above: Reconstruction of the Piltdown skull. Tests in 1949 showed that the skull was not prehistoric after all. It had been faked from an orangutan's lower jawbone and human bones of medieval origin, boiled and stained to look more ancient.

NAME
THE TRUTH?

A number of people came under suspicion as being the creator of the fake fossil. One suspect was Dawson, who was known to have faked fossils. Another was Martin Hinton, who worked at the Natural History Museum. Hinton had made tests on bone-stains, but was he a hoaxer or a detective? Hinton and Dawson may have conspired to fool Sir Arthur Smith Woodward of the Museum. Writer and fossil-hunter Sir Arthur Conan Doyle was another suspect. It was thought he may have been keen to get his own back on scientists who had ridiculed his high-profile interest in ghosts, spirits and the afterlife.

CASE CLOSED

Right and below:
Sketches of Piltdown Man, based on reconstructions published in 1913, when scientists were persuaded that Charles Dawson had unearthed a genuine "missing link" in human evolution.

Bottom: Discoverers and diggers pose at the discovery site near Piltdown in Sussex, southern England.

THE TURIN SHROUD

A holy relic from the tomb of Jesus Christ, or a skilful medieval fake? The Turin Shroud has kept its secret for centuries.

Left: A replica of the kind of tomb in which Jesus was buried, as described by his followers, with the entrance stone rolled away.

Above: This reconstruction of the tomb of Jesus includes a burial cloth. The Turin Shroud is held by some to be evidence of Christ's death and resurrection, and by others to be quite the contrary.

The Shroud is a long strip of linen cloth measuring 4.4 m (14 ft 3 in.) by 1.1 m (3 ft 7 in.). Preserved in Turin Cathedral in Italy, it is believed by some Christians to be the burial cloth in which the body of Christ was wrapped in the tomb. Its early history is itself shrouded in mystery. We know that there were reports of a sacred burial cloth in Constantinople until 1204. According to legend, the Crusaders took this shroud to France, where the first-known owner was Geoffroi de Charny, in the mid-1300s. In 1432 it was presented by his granddaughter to the Duke of Savoy. In 1532 the Shroud was damaged by fire, and repaired by some nuns, and since 1578 it has been in Turin Cathedral. Interest in the Shroud's mysterious image increased after 1898, when it was first photographed. It was noticed that the negative showed a clear image of the back and front of a man, seemingly imprinted on the cloth. On examination, the body appeared to show signs of a violent death—blows to the face, bloodstains and puncture marks on the head, lash wheals on chest and abdomen, bruising and cuts on shoulders and knees, and evidence of wounds in the wrists, feet and side. In 1902 it was suggested that the image was the imprint of a human body.

Many people became convinced that the Turin Shroud was a unique relic. German writer Karl Bernan suggested that the cloth marks might mean that Christ had been taken down from the cross alive and revived in the tomb—counter to Christian belief that Christ rose from the dead. Sceptics declared that the Shroud must be a forgery, but how it could have been made was a puzzle. The Catholic Church opposed scientific tests, for fear of damaging the fabric, but in the 1980s radiocarbon dating of the cloth was finally sanctioned.

1578 - LA S. SINDONE A TORINO - 1978
I.P.S. ROMA 1978
ITALIA   L. 220
T. MELE

Above: In 1578, a fresco of the Shroud was made by Giovanni Testa showing the Shroud on display to the Church in Turin.

FILE

Below: Detail of the head of the man whose body-image appears on the Shroud.

Above: The memorial brass on the tomb of Geoffroi de Charny (1300–1356), a French knight and the first authenticated owner of the Turin Shroud.

EVIDENCE

NAME

In 1987, laboratories in Arizona, Oxford and Zurich each tested samples of cloth from the Turin Shroud to establish its age. Their findings indicated a likely date for the linen of between 1260 and 1390. This evidence suggests the Shroud is medieval, and not from the time of Christ 2,000 years ago.

MARCH APRIL MAY JUNE

1204 ONWARD

Above: Evidence suggests that the Turin Shroud could have been woven on a Roman loom similar to this. On the other hand, an attested burial cloth from a 1st-century tomb found near Jerusalem in 2000 had a simpler weave.

Below: Pilgrims from all over the world—both clerical, like these friars, and laypeople—come to see the Turin Shroud.

Originally, it was decided that seven laboratories would test the fabric. Then the Catholic Church changed its mind, and only three were permitted to: at Oxford, Zurich and Tucson. They used fragments from a single portion of the cloth. Also contrary to the agreed protocols, the labs did not test simultaneously. Critics of the date-findings suggested that the sample was a medieval repair, or that the cloth samples had been contaminated (perhaps by smoke), distorting the carbon-date. Giulio Fanti, of the University of Padua, claims his thread-tests show a date from 300 BC to AD 400, placing the Shroud from the time of Christ. Plant pollen traces in the Shroud show links to the Jerusalem area, and while science has cast doubt on the age of the cloth, if it was made in the Middle Ages, it is an amazingly clever and mystifying fake.

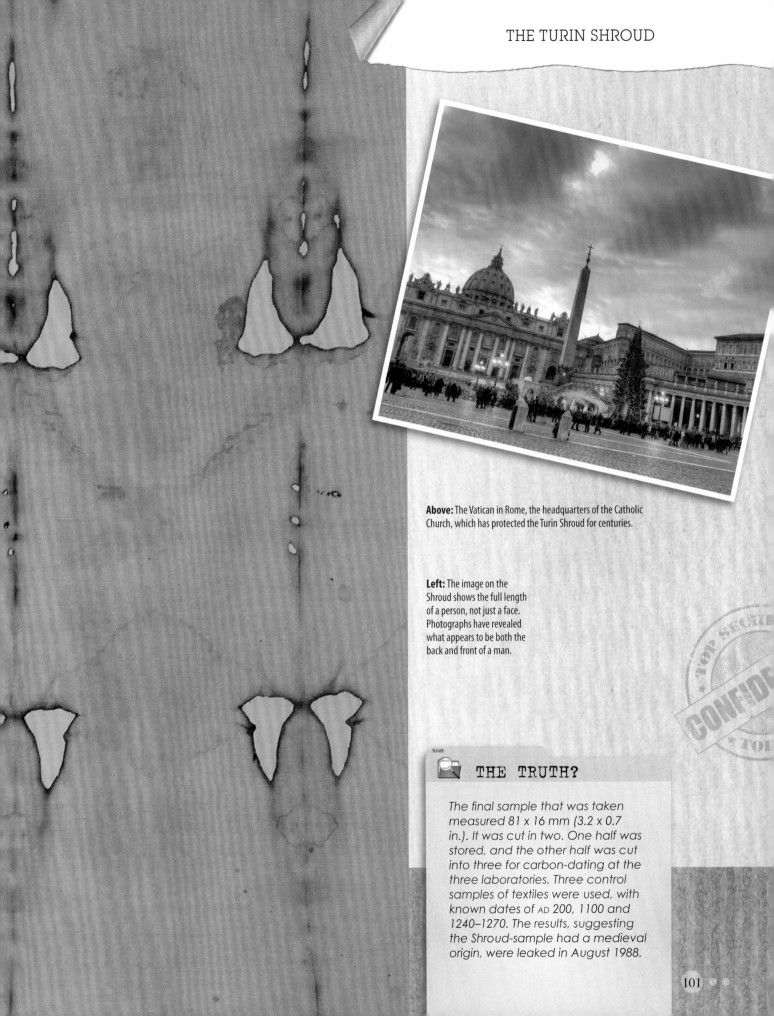

Above: The Vatican in Rome, the headquarters of the Catholic Church, which has protected the Turin Shroud for centuries.

Left: The image on the Shroud shows the full length of a person, not just a face. Photographs have revealed what appears to be both the back and front of a man.

THE TRUTH?

The final sample that was taken measured 81 x 16 mm (3.2 x 0.7 in.). It was cut in two. One half was stored, and the other half was cut into three for carbon-dating at the three laboratories. Three control samples of textiles were used, with known dates of AD 200, 1100 and 1240–1270. The results, suggesting the Shroud-sample had a medieval origin, were leaked in August 1988.

JUNE *1832*

THE YETI

High in the world's highest mountains lives the elusive Yeti, also known as the "abominable snowman." Or does it?

Stories of "wild men of the woods" abound, but the Yeti (if it exists) has a particularly inaccessible habitat – the high Himalayas. The first known European report of a Yeti was in 1832, when a British official in Nepal described an unknown hairy creature that walked erect. In 1921, the name "abominable snowman" was coined by Western climbers, striving to conquer the world's greatest mountain peaks and enthralled by local tales of the "Yeti," also called Minka or "wild man" and Kang-Admi or "snow man."

In 1948, a Norwegian claimed he'd been attacked by two Yetis in Sikkim. In 1951, British climber Eric Shipton took photos of Yeti footprints in the snow in the Gauri Sankar range. Most experts concluded the prints were those of a bear, possibly distorted as the snow melted. Local sherpas were happy to recount stories of the Yeti, and monks in a Himalayan monastery showed off Yeti bones, skins and scalps, and even a thumb. Edmund Hillary and Tenzing Norgay saw strange footprints in 1953, during the first ascent of Everest, though both remained sceptics. An expedition mounted in 1960 by Hillary failed to find proof of the Yeti's existence.

Some people speculate that tiny populations of prehistoric primates such as *Gigantopithecus* might have found sanctuary in the high Himalayas, far from people, and suggest the North American Bigfoot as a similar "wild man" survivor. Few scientists give this theory credit, though, and most believe Yetis are more likely bears, monkeys, foxes or snow leopards.

Right: An unidentified footprint, photographed in 1951 by British climbers Eric Shipton and Michael Ward in the Himalayas. The ice ax shows the footprint's size. This photo helped set off a Yeti craze.

FILE

Above: In 1954 the *Daily Mail* sponsored an expedition to search for the Yeti. The team included respected scientists, journalists and local sherpas. Sadly, no "wild man" was found.

Right: Himalayan monks preserve what some people claim are Yeti body parts. This scalp of a Yeti is kept under lock and key at Khumjung monastery in Nepal.

THE TRUTH?

In 2008, DNA analysis of supposed Yeti hair collected in the remote hills of northeast India showed it came not from a Yeti but from the Himalayan goral, a goat-like animal of the mountains. Later that year, a team of Japanese adventurers took photographs of footprints which could allegedly have been made by a Yeti, and they remain determined to film the elusive creature.

MARCH APRIL MAY JUNE *1920s ONWARD*

BIGFOOT

Do large, hairy creatures really lurk in the woods of North America? Numerous hunts for Bigfoot have failed to find the hairy wild men.

Above: Hapless hoax or hairy hominid, Bigfoot has set his feet firmly into some tracts of North American culture – even to the extent of inspiring warning signs on highways!

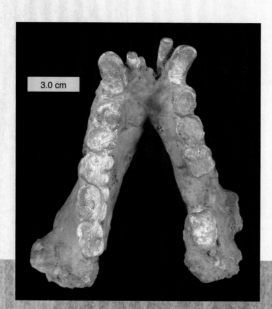

Below: The fossil jaw of the extinct primate *Gigantopithecus blacki*. Some Bigfoot proponents have suggested that sightings of Bigfoot could be relict populations of this giant prehistoric ape-man.

3.0 cm

Bigfoot is supposed to haunt the forests of the American and Canadian Northwest. Said to be 2–3 m (6–10 ft) tall, heavier than a man, with huge feet, shaggy hair and a repulsive smell, its other name is Sasquatch, from a First Nation/Native American word *sasq'ets*. The Sasquatch first hit the press in Canada in the 1920s, after sensational stories were reported of miners and monsters in the woods. One miner claimed he'd been abducted by a Bigfoot, and another that he and his companions were attacked by ape-men hurling rocks. The stories were dismissed as hoaxes or practical jokes, possibly played by student campers.

More reports of sightings and footprints were made during the 1950s, along with further hoax allegations. Bigfoot paw-prints found at Bluff Creek, California, in 1958, were made by wooden feet, according to the family of Bigfoot-hunter and hoaxer Raymond Wallace (1918–2002), who is known to have faked Bigfoot hair using the hair from a bison.

Of hundreds of Bigfoot sightings, the most famous was in 1967, filmed by Roger Patterson and Robert Gimlin at Eureka, California. Captured on 16 mm (0.6 in.) film is what looks like a hairy female humanoid, walking erect and swinging its arms before hurrying off into the woods. The film aroused great excitement, and violent arguments. Did the film show a genuine "cryptid" or unknown animal, or was it a hoax? Bob Heironimus, a friend of Patterson's, later said Bigfoot was really him in an ape-suit, but Patterson and Gimlin refused to own up. Bigfoot was also spotted further east, in Illinois, where in 1973 a couple in a parked car were scared out of their wits by a roaring, hairy, slime-dripping creature that entered local folklore as the Murphysboro Mud Monster. The foul smell they described seemed to show affinities with the Sasquatch!

Above: A map of North America showing where people claim to have spotted Bigfoot. The darkest areas indicate the highest number of sightings.

Right: The most famous Bigfoot sighting was staged by a man in a hairy ape-suit!

 NAME

EVIDENCE?

Photographs taken in 2007 of a mysterious hairy primate were, according to scientists, most likely to be a bear with mange, though some suggested the limbs looked more like a chimpanzee's. In 2008 a YouTube video claimed to show a dead Bigfoot, found in Georgia. TV networks clustered around the frozen corpse in its freezer, but it turned out to be just another hoax, with a hollow head and rubber feet!

Many cultures have tales of wild men and giants, some shy and harmless, others flesh-eating ogres that carry off women and children. But there are no great apes in North America's fossil record!

CONFIDENTIAL
★ TOP SECRET

UNKNOWN ANIMALS

Species new to science are still being discovered, but none so outlandish as the weird and wonderful beasts of legend!

Some "unknown animals," the Yeti for instance, seem more like humans. Elusive "little men" are said to haunt remote forests and mountains, for example the orang pendek of Sumatra, or the nittaewo of Sri Lanka. Sceptics point out that their footprints are more likely those of bears or monkeys, but the "little men" remind others of the prehistoric mini-people, real life "hobbits" known to have lived alongside early humans. Less credible maybe is the di-di, a South American ape-man with flowing hair but only one leg, progressing in giant hops. Hopping men are usually linked with the supernatural. In the 1850s, villagers in Devon, England, woke to gasp at strange footprints in the snow criss-crossing walls and roofs—tracks that passed into local legend as the "Devil's hoofmarks."

The medieval imagination created all kinds of bestiary animals. The fabled unicorn was difficult to hunt (in stories, only a virgin could soothe it), but unicorn-hide shoes were said to ward off the plague, and the horn was an antidote to poison—so fake "unicorn horn" (from rhino or narwhal) was expensive. The closest nature comes to the unicorn is the Arabian oryx.

Strange tales were brought back by explorers of bizarre creatures, such as the Brazilian minhocao, a monstrous two-horned worm; or the African chepweke, a lizard 13 m (45 ft) long, which killed elephants and hippos! Another swamp-monster, the fabled Australian bunyip, chewed up people, while the Maoris of New Zealand were wary of the taniwha, a supernatural shape-changer both protective and dangerous, carrying off women.

Above: Ureia, a guardian taniwha, a mythical sea creature that could protect or turn nasty. This one is carved on a house post inside a Maori meeting house built in 1878 in New Zealand.

Below right: The mysterious Devil's hoofmarks were thought by some people to have been made by jumping wood mice.

AT A GLANCE

NAME

In 1812 the eminent scientist Baron Cuvier declared that no new large animals were likely to be found, science having already named the main species. In fact, new animals, though rarely large, are found all the time, recent examples being the Annamite striped rabbit in Laos, the Australian snubfin dolphin, the Bornean clouded leopard, and the Welsh ghost slug, which is white and eats worms.

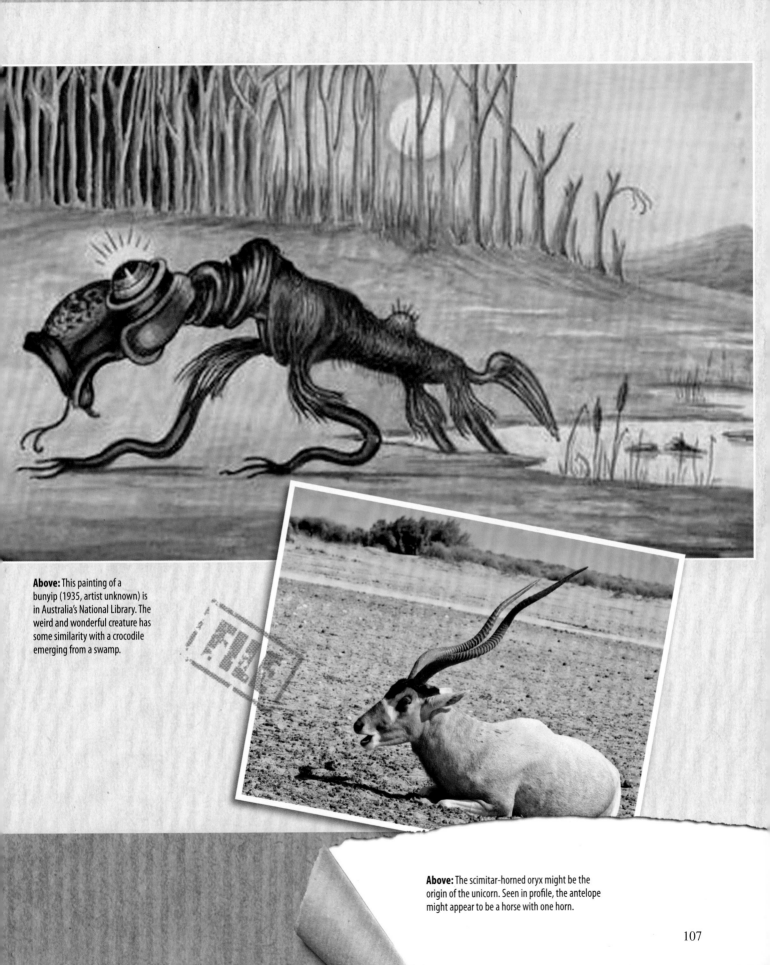

Above: This painting of a bunyip (1935, artist unknown) is in Australia's National Library. The weird and wonderful creature has some similarity with a crocodile emerging from a swamp.

Above: The scimitar-horned oryx might be the origin of the unicorn. Seen in profile, the antelope might appear to be a horse with one horn.

JANUARY FEBRUARY MARCH **APRIL 1934**

Above: A postcard of Loch Ness bearing the words "The haunts of the Monster" invites tourists to peer closer.

Below: Many visitors are drawn to Loch Ness hoping to catch a glimpse of something strange swimming in the loch.

THE LOCH NESS MONSTER

Loch Ness in Scotland is more than 300 m (900 ft) deep. In 1934, a London doctor on holiday took a photograph of a snaky neck and head protruding from the peaty waters. The picture of a "monster" caused a sensation.

More sightings followed, such as when local resident Lachlan Stuart, up early for morning milking in 1951, spotted three humps. In 1960, Tim Dinsdale shot the first moving pictures of "Nessie," and in 1961 the Loch Ness Phenomena Investigation Bureau set up observers and cameras around the loch to try and establish if there really were creatures lurking in its murky depths.

Nessie remained unseen until, in 1975, Robert Rines produced film that convinced naturalist Peter Scott that there was a genuine unknown species: it appeared reddish-brown, about 4 m (13 ft) long and had an arching neck and flippers. Could a small population of prehistoric plesiosaurs have survived in Loch Ness? After all, there were tales of other Scottish lake beasts, such as the Mhorag of Loch Morar,

The Rines images sparked worldwide interest, though geologists ridiculed any pre-Ice Age survivor theory. Sonar scans picked up occasional unidentified tracks or objects, but, in 2003, a survey for the BBC using sonar and satellite technology found nothing. Images continued to surface. In 2007, Gordon Holmes videoed "something about 13 m (45 ft) long," though this sighting was challenged, as was a 2011 photo of something trailing a boat, dismissed by sceptics as a mass of weed. In 2008, Dr Rines concluded that Nessie might be extinct. Without a body, the Loch Ness Monster remains, in Scottish legal terms, "not proven."

NAME

EVIDENCE?

Dr George Zug, reptile expert at the Smithsonian Institution in the United States, gave his opinion of the Rines images: "I believe these data indicate the presence of large animals in Loch Ness, but are insufficient to identify them." It seems unlikely that any large animals, prehistoric or modern, could thrive in Loch Ness, unless swimming in and out through subterranean rivers to the sea. Prosaic explanations for the Loch Ness monster include decaying plant matter, waves and water eddies, and mistaken sightings of seals or otters.

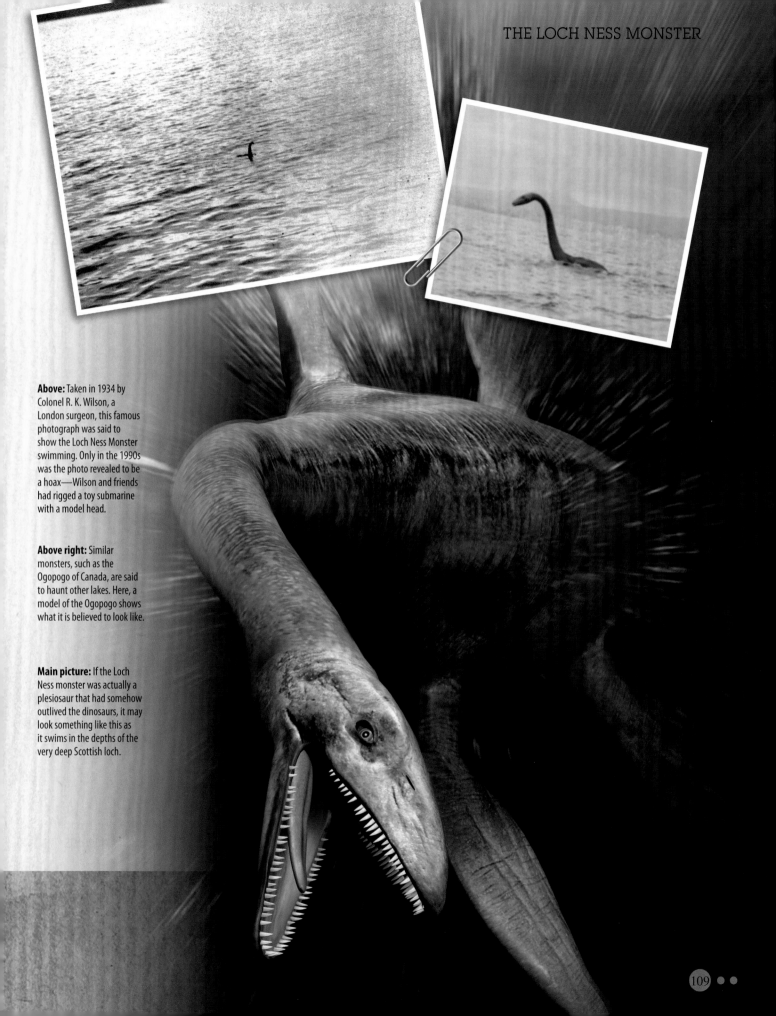

Above: Taken in 1934 by Colonel R. K. Wilson, a London surgeon, this famous photograph was said to show the Loch Ness Monster swimming. Only in the 1990s was the photo revealed to be a hoax—Wilson and friends had rigged a toy submarine with a model head.

Above right: Similar monsters, such as the Ogopogo of Canada, are said to haunt other lakes. Here, a model of the Ogopogo shows what it is believed to look like.

Main picture: If the Loch Ness monster was actually a plesiosaur that had somehow outlived the dinosaurs, it may look something like this as it swims in the depths of the very deep Scottish loch.

MARCH APRIL MAY JUNE *JULY 1917*

FAIRIES AT THE BOTTOM OF THE GARDEN

Above: Frances Griffiths and Elsie Wright, taken in 1917 by Arthur Wright on his new "Midg" plate camera. The picture was published in 1922 in Sir Arthur Conan Doyle's *The Coming of the Fairies*.

In July 1917, two girls in a Yorkshire village took photographs of the fairies in their garden. For many years people wondered if the Cottingley fairies were really evidence of another world, or simply a children's prank.

Cousins Elsie Wright (16) and Frances Griffiths (10) were at the Wrights' home in Cottingley, near Bradford, Yorkshire, when they got wet playing by the stream. They gave the excuse that they'd been "playing with fairies," and to prove it persuaded Elsie's father to lend them his new camera.

The first photograph showed Frances with four fairies. Weeks later the girls took a photograph of Elsie with a gnome. In 1919 Mrs Wright showed the fairy pictures to the local Theosophical Society in Bradford. As a Theosophist, Mrs Wright was inclined toward a belief in a spirit-world; in the years following the mass slaughter of the First World War, many people had turned toward such beliefs. Fellow-Theosophist Edward Gardner believed he was looking at photographic evidence of "spiritual evolution", and in the summer of 1920 he asked the girls to try again. With a different camera, the girls took three new pictures, unobserved by adults: the first showed Frances with a leaping fairy; the second showed Elsie being offered flowers by a fairy; and the third was a picture of "Fairies and their Sun-Bath."

The photos caused much excitement. In 1921, the writer and spiritualist Sir Arthur Conan Doyle, of *Sherlock Holmes* fame, published the Cottingley photographs in an article on fairies in the *Strand Magazine*. He went on to write a book about them. Gardner and clairvoyant Geoffrey Hodson tried again, but no fairies came out to be photographed, and the girls later admitted having fun at Hodson's expense.

CASE CLOSED

A. ALICE AND THE FAIRIES.
Copyright. Photograph taken July, 1917.

Above: Frances with four fairies, in the first of the Cottingley fairy photographs.

Photography experts argued about the fairy photos. Could the fairies possibly be genuine? Sceptics pointed out that they looked too much like "illustrated fairies", with fashionable hairstyles. Supporters could not believe that eminent people such as Conan Doyle could be taken in by children.

THE TRUTH?

Gardner and Conan Doyle asked Kodak experts to validate the fairy photos. The verdict was that, although there were no obvious signs of faking, the images were not necessarily of real fairies. Since there were no such things as fairies, a Kodak technician suggested, the photos must be faked "somehow".

Above: Cottingley Beck waterfall in Yorkshire, where the girls claimed they saw their fairies.

MARCH APRIL MAY JUNE JULY 1917

The girls grew up, married, lived abroad and were almost forgotten, until, in the 1980s, they were interviewed again—and changed their story. They admitted the fairies were a joke, which they'd been amazed to find taken seriously. They had cut the fairies from a children's book, fixed them in position with hatpins, then photographed them. Elsie maintained, however, that one photo (the fifth) was indeed genuine.

50

Left: Elsie is offered a posy of flowers by a fairy. This photograph was taken by Frances during the second episode of fairy photos.

Left: The photograph was taken on this camera, which was provided by Edward Gardner.

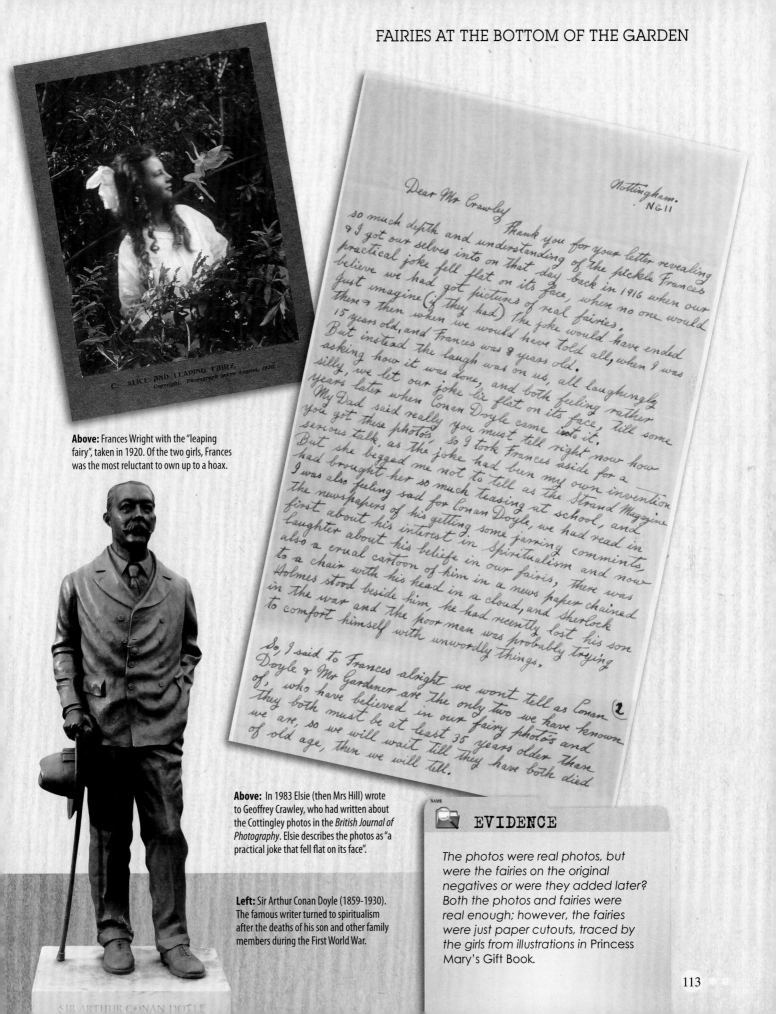

Above: Frances Wright with the "leaping fairy", taken in 1920. Of the two girls, Frances was the most reluctant to own up to a hoax.

Dear Mr Crawley

Nottingham. NG11

Thank you for your letter revealing so much depth and understanding of the pickle Frances & I got our selves into on that day back in 1916 when our practical joke fell flat on its face, when no one would believe we had got pictures of real fairies.

Just imagine (if they had) the joke would have ended there → then when we would have told all, when I was 15 years old, and Frances was 9 years old.

But instead the laugh was on us, all laughingly asking how it was done, and both feeling rather silly, we let our joke lie flat on its face, till some years later when Conan Doyle came into it.

My Dad said really you must tell right now how you got these photos', so I took Frances aside for a serious talk, as the joke had been my own invention. But she begged me not to tell as the Strand Magazine had brought her so much teasing at school, and I was also feeling sad for Conan Doyle, we had read in the newspapers of his getting some jarring comments, first about his interest in Spiritualism and now laughter about his belief in our fairies, there was also a cruel cartoon of him in a news paper chained to a chair with his head in a cloud, and Sherlock Holmes stood beside him, he had recently lost his son in the war and the poor man was probably trying to comfort himself with unwordly things.

So, I said to Frances alright we wont tell as Conan Doyle & Mr Gardener are the only two we have known of, who have believed in our fairy photo's and they both must be at least 35 years older than we are, so we will wait till they have both died of old age, then we will tell. (2)

Above: In 1983 Elsie (then Mrs Hill) wrote to Geoffrey Crawley, who had written about the Cottingley photos in the *British Journal of Photography*. Elsie describes the photos as "a practical joke that fell flat on its face".

Left: Sir Arthur Conan Doyle (1859-1930). The famous writer turned to spiritualism after the deaths of his son and other family members during the First World War.

NAME

📇 EVIDENCE

The photos were real photos, but were the fairies on the original negatives or were they added later? Both the photos and fairies were real enough; however, the fairies were just paper cutouts, traced by the girls from illustrations in Princess Mary's Gift Book.

MARCH APRIL MAY JUNE *1842*

THE FEEJEE MERMAID

The mermaid of myth is beautiful and often wistful, but the mermaids exhibited at fairs and freak shows were a very different kettle of fish.

Mermaids in folklore are half-woman, half-fish, though in some tales they can live on land, and even become human. Mermaids and mermen were rather like fairies: magical but not immortal, without souls but drawn to people, sometimes fatally. Mermaids' songs could lure sailors to their dooms, though a man might marry a mermaid and keep her if he stole her comb and mirror, or her cap and belt. So long as he kept them hidden, his mermaid-lover would remain with him.

A celebrated medieval mermaid was said to have been found in 1403 on mudflats at Edam in Holland. Befriended by village women, she lived 15 years and was given a Christian burial in the churchyard, but never learned to speak. Cornwall is particularly rich in mermaid stories, such as the Mermaid of Zennor, who fell in love with a local man.

Not surprisingly, hoaxers and charlatans cashed in with fake mermaids that in most cases looked so hideous that few people could have been convinced by them. Taxidermists and showmen combined to wow the public with grotesque creations put together from bits of fish, lizard, pig and monkey. In the 19th century, Japanese fishermen did a flourishing trade selling dead fish-monkey mermaids. Perhaps the most celebrated mermaid was displayed by American impresario and circus man P. T. Barnum in 1842. Advertised as the "Feejee Mermaid," and purportedly caught by a Dr Griffin, the exhibit toured country shows and fairs across the United States. It was later acquired by Harvard University's Peabody Museum of Archaeology and Ethnology. The mummified mermaid turned out to be just another shrivelled fake.

Above: Phineas T. Barnum (1810–1891), whose attractions included General Tom Thumb and Jumbo the elephant. He once claimed to have exhibited George Washington's nurse.

Below: The Banff Merman is kept in a glass case at the Canadian city's Indian Trading Post. A shipping bill suggests the store's former owner bought a "man-fish" from Java, but it may well have been a home-made hoax.

Above: A statue of Syrene, a war-like mermaid in Warsaw's Market Square, originally created in 1850 to echo the mermaid on the city's coat of arms.

NAME

THE TRUTH?

Sailors came home with stories of strange sea monsters, none more terrifying than the Kraken, as big as an island, with tentacles that dragged down ships. The giant squid can grow to vast size but lives in the ocean deeps and, despite its starring role in films such as 20,000 Leagues Under the Sea, is unlikely to wrestle with a ship!

Above: The un-alluring Feejee Mermaid, a grisly composite of paper, glue, stuffing, fish-tail, baby orangutan and monkey-head, dried and crinkled.

OCTOBER 1869

THE CARDIFF GIANT

Stories of giants and ogres are found in many cultures. The Cardiff Giant became a brief sensation in 1869. But what was the truth?

The Cardiff Giant was found a long way from Wales, in Cardiff, New York State. Workers digging a well on land owned by William C. Newell dug up a stone man 3 m (10 ft) tall. Farmer Newell, known to friends as "Stub," was soon charging sightseers 50 cents a time to gaze upon the petrified person.

Who or what was the Cardiff Giant? Some Christian folk turned to their Bibles and held that the giant was one of those mentioned in the Book of Genesis. Others thought it might be an extinct mega-human, fossilized by nature or turned to stone by witchcraft. Some declared the giant to be a statue made by early Christian missionaries to awe the local Indians.

In fact, the giant was soon revealed to be a hoax. The hoaxer was George Hull, an atheist who may have relished a joke against the Bible-belt, in collusion with farmer Newell and the stonemasons Hull hired to craft his scam. Hull had the giant figure buried secretly on Newell's farm in November 1868. He waited a year, until all the locals had forgotten seeing a creaking heavy-laden wagon with a mysterious covered load, then the "well-digging" commenced in October 1869, and Newell's neighbors duly uncovered the giant as planned. Hull recouped his expenses, and more, when some local worthies offered to buy the giant and exhibit it at the city of Syracuse.

Showman P. T. Barnum made a bid for the giant, was refused, and so displayed a plaster copy instead, and the copy was soon drawing even bigger crowds than the original giant, which now resides in the Farmers' Museum at Cooperstown in New York State.

Above: Fossil expert Othniel C. Marsh, famous dinosaur-hunter, exposed the Cardiff Giant as a fake. Hull tried the same stunt with a second giant, in Colorado, but it fooled nobody.

Below: A stonemason's chisel was pretty much all Hull needed to create his giant, plus some willing hands to craft, transport and excavate it.

NAME

THE TRUTH?

The Cardiff Giant was cut from soft rock called gypsum. The rock wasn't difficult to carve, but transporting it posed problems, since the massive gypsum block weighed 2 tons. The finished giant was made to look more realistic by pricking its stone "skin" with needles to make pore marks.

Above: This photograph from 1869 shows the rig over the site from which the astounding petrified giant was purportedly exhumed.

Left: A poster for Barnum and Bailey's famous circus. Barnum was always on the lookout for new attractions, the bigger the better.

NOVEMBER DECEMBER **JANUARY 2000**

THE MILLENNIUM BUG

The Y2K or Year 2000 problem caused worldwide mini-hysteria. Would computers crash? If so, would the world as we know it end, or at least slow down?

Computers mark time on internal clocks and calendars. Customarily, 20th-century computers abbreviated a year date to 2 digits (so 1998 = 98). As the end of the 20th century approached, what would happen to computers as the year 99 rolled over to 00? As the Millennium Bug popped its head above the cyber-wall, there was talk of "nasty shocks" and the "Y2K" problem. Fears were raised of "holes" in military networks, breakdowns in banking and retail, even fuel and food shortages.

As the "main event horizon," January 1, 2000, approached, the global e-community seemed split between those scared that the end of the e-world was nigh, and those who dismissed the Millennium Bug as scaremongering, hoax, or a criminal conspiracy opening the way for cyber-attacks on bank accounts. When the New Year dawned, the Y2K effect was minimal, with only minor problems, such as alarms going off, mobile phones deleting new messages instead of old ones, and master clocks going wrong. The US Naval Observatory clock, for instance, gave the date on its website as Jan 1, 19100. In the event, most computers were already Y2K-compliant, and carried on. The Internet did not collapse.

The Y2K panic again showed the power of the Internet to disseminate hoax and conspiracy stories. For instance, in 1994 Internet "reports" claimed Microsoft boss Bill Gates had acquired exclusive e-rights to the Bible! In the event, the Bug was no threat. Most systems were fine simply by being restarted, and by Jan 1, 2000, the snowball story had melted away and the e-world was still in place.

Above: In the days before January 1, 2000, the US Federal Reserve was seriously worried about a flood of withdrawals by people fearful that atm machines would be hit by the Millennium Bug.

SUSPECT

EVIDENCE

The United States passed an Act of Congress to "be ready" for Y2K problems, and federal agencies set up Y2K task forces. Insurance companies cashed in by selling policies covering failures caused by the Bug. Groups anticipating the end of the world stocked up on canned and dried food—just in case the lights went out.

SM 75|2

Top and above: Airlines reassured passengers that air traffic control radar and air safety were not at risk. Even so, as the world's clock ticked toward midnight and 1999's end, many passengers were more anxious than usual.

Below right: Computers hold so much of our personal information. People were worried that all that data might suddenly become inaccessible, or simply vanish!

MARCH APRIL MAY JUNE 1978

Above: ET just landed. This drawing of "an alien spaceship spotted making crop circles" was sent to UK government military experts to examine in the late 1990s.

Below: Best seen from the air, this crop formation was photographed in Diessenhofen, Switzerland, in July 2008.

EVIDENCE

NAME

The Nazca lines in Peru are best seen from the air, yet were made between 100 BC and AD 800, long before aircraft. On the ground can be seen giant figures of spiders, fish, lizards and other animals, as well as geometric shapes. Why did the Nazca people draw them with such precision and effort? Possibly they wanted to communicate with sky-gods, or they may have been fertility symbols or calendars.

CROP CIRCLES

What makes circular patterns in wheat fields? Some people like to believe that UFOs are responsible. Others suggest they are the work of followers of ancient religions, while some are simply made by artistic hoaxers.

Crop circles are geometric patterns, sometimes intricate and very large (over 200 m/650 ft) across. They are best seen from the air.

Formations that looked regular, even artistic, were first seen in fields of cereal crops in the 1970s. At first, they were associated with UFO landings or with unexplained other-worldly phenomena. Was it significant that so many crop circles were made in the ritual landscape of England, close to the ancient Bronze Age sites of Stonehenge and Avebury? However, similar phenomena have been reported in other countries. In Indonesia, crop circles were ruled to be "pseudoscience" (and so possibly alien), while the Australians blamed wallabies running in circles after grazing on opium-rich poppies!

Significantly, crop circles do not appear in medieval folklore, nor in Victorian scientists' accounts of rural beliefs and old customs. In the 1980s, meteorologists speculated that freak winds could flatten crops by "vortex-action." Ufologists claimed crop circles were made by alien spacecraft, possibly in an attempt to communicate. Another theory suggested crop circles were the Earth "talking to us"—an expression of a mysterious "Earth force," as yet unknown to science.

Human hoaxers are, however, the most obvious cause of crop circles. Two chief suspects, Doug Bower and Dave Chorley, claimed they started making circles in England in 1978 and went on to create over 200. Soon crop formations were seen in other countries. Since the 1980s there have been crop-circle competitions and even TV demonstrations of how to make one!

CASE CLOSED

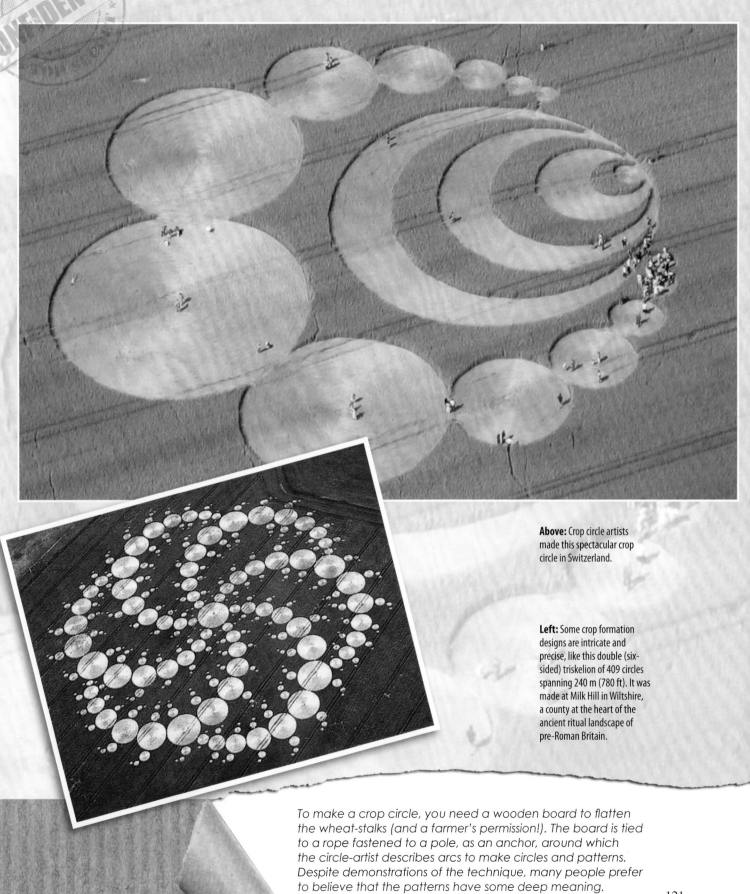

Above: Crop circle artists made this spectacular crop circle in Switzerland.

Left: Some crop formation designs are intricate and precise, like this double (six-sided) triskelion of 409 circles spanning 240 m (780 ft). It was made at Milk Hill in Wiltshire, a county at the heart of the ancient ritual landscape of pre-Roman Britain.

To make a crop circle, you need a wooden board to flatten the wheat-stalks (and a farmer's permission!). The board is tied to a rope fastened to a pole, as an anchor, around which the circle-artist describes arcs to make circles and patterns. Despite demonstrations of the technique, many people prefer to believe that the patterns have some deep meaning.

AVIATION

Airplane accidents are far less common than road accidents, but a plane crash always make news.

Usually the cause of tragedy is clear cut, but confusion and conspiracy shrouds some of the most celebrated disasters in the annals of aviation. Investigators pore over mangled wreckage, seeking to establish the truth, amid an ongoing media and internet discussion of possible causes and conspiracy suspects. Conspiracy allegations have been aired about the fate of two airliners in recent decades: TWA Flight 800 and Pan Am Flight 103, whose stories are told here. The loss of any modern plane is a shock, but in the early years of aviation every trans-ocean flight was full of risk. The disappearance of a pioneer flier made headlines, and aroused speculation—none more so than when the world's most famous "fallen flier", US aviatrix extraordinaire Amelia Earhart, set off across the Pacific in 1937, never to be seen again.

26A

26A

MARCH APRIL MAY JUNE **JULY 1996**

TWA FLIGHT 800

On July 17, 1996, TWA Flight 800 left New York for Paris. Eleven minutes after take-off it plummeted into the Atlantic Ocean. All 230 people aboard died—victims of a tragic accident or a missile strike?

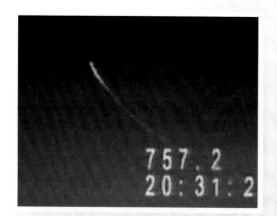

Above: An NTSB animation shows what witnesses may have seen after a fuel tank on the plane's left wing exploded. The front of the aircraft broke off but flew on for some 30 seconds. The reported "missile trail" was the plane's rear section in flames.

Below: In this FBI witness statement regarding the accident, a woman describes how she saw what looked like a boat flare moving across the sky.

In June 2013 a TV documentary re-aired the Flight 800 controversy. Former crash investigators refuted the official verdict, insisting there had been an explosion outside the aircraft, not inside. There were reports that people had seen a missile. Or was it a bomb? According to the authorities, Flight 800 was brought down by internal electrical failure that caused a fire.

TWA Flight 800 left JFK airport in New York for Paris. The aircraft was a Boeing 747, one of the early 1971-series. About 32 km (20 mi.) southwest of East Hampton, New York, it was blown apart. Some witnesses (one a Vietnam veteran pilot) claimed to have seen a missile trail. Had Flight 800 been shot down by terrorists? No terrorists claimed responsibility. Three US Navy submarines and a missile-cruiser were in the vicinity. Had a test-fired missile hit the 747 by mistake? Why the media blackout, and were the authorities hiding the facts to avoid passenger-panic?

Parallels were drawn with Pan Am Flight 103, blown up by a terrorist bomb over Scotland in 1988. Had Flight 800 been brought down by a bomb? There were allegations that crash investigators found explosive residues under seats in the wreck. The authorities insisted that any explosive traces were left over from routine training exercises with sniffer dogs taught to detect bombs.

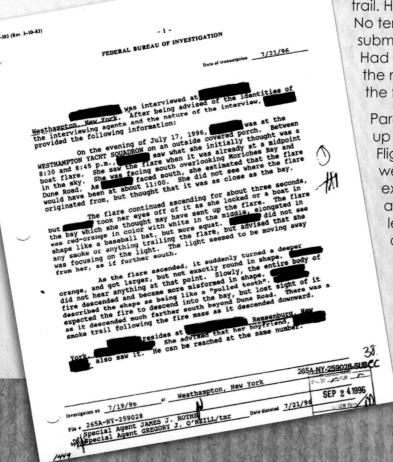

THE TRUTH?

After a four-year investigation, the US National Transportation Safety Board (NTSB) rejected the missile/ bomb hypothesis, deciding that an electrical short-circuit in the plane's fuel system wiring started a fire that ignited full tanks of inflammable aviation fuel. The NTSB issued 15 safety recommendations to improve aircraft design. Charges of a cover-up remained.

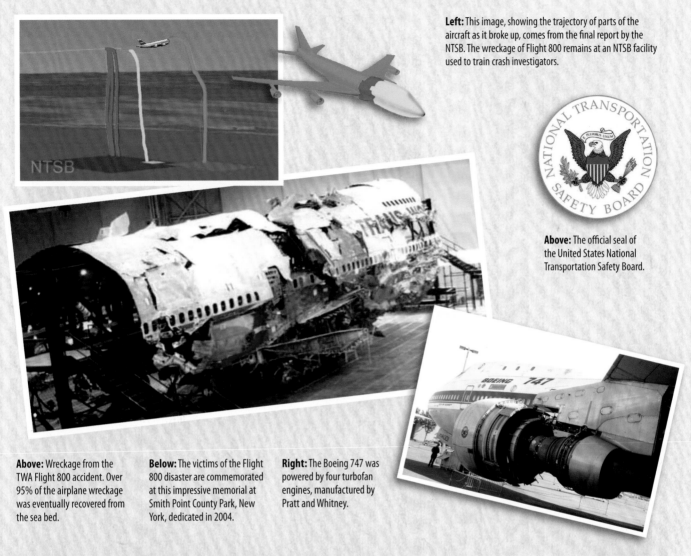

Left: This image, showing the trajectory of parts of the aircraft as it broke up, comes from the final report by the NTSB. The wreckage of Flight 800 remains at an NTSB facility used to train crash investigators.

Above: The official seal of the United States National Transportation Safety Board.

Above: Wreckage from the TWA Flight 800 accident. Over 95% of the airplane wreckage was eventually recovered from the sea bed.

Below: The victims of the Flight 800 disaster are commemorated at this impressive memorial at Smith Point County Park, New York, dedicated in 2004.

Right: The Boeing 747 was powered by four turbofan engines, manufactured by Pratt and Whitney.

DECEMBER 1988

PAN AM FLIGHT 103

Pan Am Flight 103 outward bound from London Heathrow to New York's JFK airport crashed on December 21, 1988. Ever since, there have been questions about who planted the bomb that killed 270 people.

Libya was accused, but never admitted responsibility, though it did pay compensation to victims' families. Conspiracy theorists, and some government sources, blame other culprits. US intelligence claimed Iran financed the attack, in revenge for the shooting down earlier in 1988 of an Iranian airliner by the US warship *USS Vincennes*. The terrorist Abu Nidal (killed in 2002) reportedly admitted plotting the Flight 103 disaster. The Israeli secret service Mossad and the apartheid South African government were also accused, though denied any involvement. The US Central Intelligence Agency noted that of several suspects for the terrorist attack on Flight 103, the Iranians were "the most credible so far".

One suggestion is that the bomb was intended for a Frankfurt–New York flight carrying US military personnel on Christmas leave, but was put on the wrong plane. Another possibility aired by conspiracy theorists is that the CIA was operating a "protected drugs route" for Syrian drug-traffickers to fly in and out of the US in exchange for information about Palestinian organizations; according to this theory, the bomb was taken on board Flight 103 by a "drugs mule", by mistake, or deliberately as a suicide attack. If the CIA knew, they kept quiet because it was a rogue operation, but this theory has little evidence to support it.

Above: A propaganda poster showing Colonel Muammar al-Gaddafi in Tripoli.

Below: Pan Am Flight 103 exploded over the town of Lockerbie in Scotland. If the bomb had gone off a short while later, over the Atlantic, all evidence would most likely have been lost.

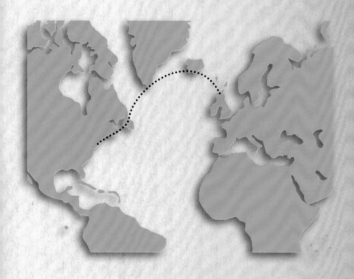

NAME

THE TRUTH?

In 1999, Libya's leader Colonel Gaddafi agreed to the trial of two Libyans in the Netherlands, though only one of them, Abdelbaset al-Megrahi, was convicted. Released from prison in 2009 with cancer, he died in Libya in 2012. In 2011, after Gaddafi's overthrow, a Libyan official said there was proof the Libyan leader had authorized al-Megrahi to bomb Flight 103.

Left: Lockerbie is a small, quiet place. The events of that day left permanent scars, on people's memories. The crash of Flight 103 killed all 259 passengers and crew, along with 11 people on the ground.

Below: The Boeing 747 was flying at 9,400 m (31,000 ft) when the aircraft was torn apart by a bomb. It broke into two sections, crashing onto the Scottish town of Lockerbie.

Left: The victims of the Lockerbie disaster are remembered on this memorial at the town cemetery.

IN REMEMBRANCE OF ALL VICTIMS
OF LOCKERBIE AIR DISASTER
WHO DIED ON 21st DECEMBER 1988

JOHN MICHAEL GERARD AHERN
SARAH MARGARET AICHER
JOHN DAVID AKERSTROM
RONALD ELY ALEXANDER
THOMAS JOSEPH AMMERMAN
MARTIN LEWIS APFELBAUM
RACHEL MARIE ABELDIN
JUDITH ELLEN ATKINSON
WILLIAM GARRETSON ATKINSON
ELISABETH NICHOLE AVOYNE
JERRY DON AVRITT
CLARE LOUISE BACCIOCHI
HARRY MICHAEL BAINBRIDGE
STUART MURRAY BARCLAY
JEAN MARY BELL
JULIAN MORGAN BENELLO
LAWRENCE RAY BENNETT
PHILIP VERNON BERGSTROM
ALISTAIR DAVID BERKLEY
MICHAEL STUART BERNSTEIN
STEVEN RUSSELL BERRELL
SURINDER MOHAN BHATIA
KENNETH JOHN BISSETT
DIANE ANN BOATMAN-FULLER
STEPHEN JOHN BOLAND
COLYN JOHN BOUCKLEY
PAULA MARIE BOUCKLEY
NICOLE ELISE BOULANGER
FRANCIS BOYER
NICHOLAS BRIGHT
DANIEL SOLOMON BROWNER BEEBY
COLLEEN RENEE BRUNNER
TIMOTHY GUY BURMAN
MICHAEL WARREN BUSER
WARREN MAX BUSER
STEVEN LEE BUTLER
WILLIAM MARTIN CADMAN
FABIANA CAFFARONE
HERNAN CAFFARONE
VALERIE CANADY
GREGORY CAPASSO
TIMOTHY MICHAEL CARDWELL
BERNT WILMAR CARLSSON
RICHARD ANTHONY CAWLEY

FRANK CIULLA
THEODORA EUGENIA COHEN
ERIC MICHAEL COKER
JASON MICHAEL COKER
GARY LEONARD COLASANTI
BRIDGET CONCANNON
SEAN CONCANNON
THOMAS CONCANNON
TRACEY JANE CORNER
SCOTT CORY
WILLIS LARRY COURSEY
PATRICIA MARY COYLE
JOHN BINNING CUMMOCK
JOSEPH PATRICK CURRY
WILLIAM ALLAN DANIELS
GRETCHEN JOYCE DATER
SHANNON DAVIS
GABRIEL DELLA-RIPA
OM DIKSHIT
SHANTI DIXIT
JOYCE CHRISTINE DIMAURO
GIANFRANCA DINARDO
PETER THOMAS STANLEY DIX
DAVID SCOTT DORNSTEIN
MICHAEL JOSEPH DOYLE
EDGAR HOWARD EGGLESTON III
SIV ULLA ENGSTROM
TURHAN ERGIN
CHARLES THOMAS FISHER IV
JOANNE FLANNIGAN
KATHLEEN MARY FLANNIGAN
THOMAS BROWN FLANNIGAN
CLAYTON LEE FLICK
JOHN PATRICK FLYNN
ARTHUR FONDILER
ROBERT GERARD FORTUNE
STACIE DENISE FRANKLIN
PAUL MATTHEW STEPHEN FREEMAN
JAMES RALPH FULLER
IBOLYA GABOR
AMY BETH GALLAGHER
MATTHEW KEVIN GANNON
KENNETH RAYMOND GARCZYNSKI
PAUL ISAAC GARRETT
KENNETH JAMES GIBSON

WILLIAM DAVID GIEBLER
ANDREW CHRISTOPHER GILLIES-WRIGHT
OLIVE LEONORA GORDON
LINDA SUSAN GORDON-GORGACZ
ANNE MADELENE GORGACZ
LORETTA ANNE GORGACZ
DAVID GOULD
LINDIE NIKOLAI GLEVCEVGIAN
NICOLA JANE HALL
LORRAINE FRANCES HALSCH
LYNNE CAROL HARTUNIAN
ANTHONY LACEY HAWKINS
DORA HENRIETTA HENRY
MAURICE PETER HENRY
PAMELA ELAINE HERBERT
RODNEY PETER HILBERT
ALFRED HILL
KATHERINE AUGUSTA HOLLISTER
JOSEPHINE LISA HUDSON
MELINA HUDSON
SOPHIE AILETTE MIRIAM HUDSON
KAREN LEE HUNT
ROGER ELWOOD HURST
ELIZABETH SOPHIE IVELL
KHALED NAZIR JAAFAR
ROBERT VAN HOUTEN JECK
PAUL AVRON JEFFREYS
RACHEL JEFFREYS
KATHLEEN MARY JERMYN
BETH ANN JOHNSON
MARY LINCOLN JOHNSON
TIMOTHY BARON JOHNSON
CHRISTOPHER ANDREW JONES
JULIANNE FRANCES KELLY
JAY JOSEPH KINGHAM
PATRICIA ANN KLEIN
GREGORY KOSMOWSKI
MINAS CHRISTOPHER KULUKUNDIS
MARY LANCASTER
RONALD ALBERT LARIVIERE
MARIA NIEVES LARRACOECHEA
ROBERT MILTON LECKBURG
WILLIAM CHASE LEYRER
ANNE LINCOLN

ALEXANDER LOWENSTEIN
LLOYD DAVID LUDLOW
MARIA THERESIA LURBKE
JAMES BRUCE MacQUARRIE
WILLIAM JOHN McALLISTER
DANIEL EMMET McCARTHY
ROBERT EUGENE McCOLLUM
CHARLES DENNIS McKEE
BERNARD JOSEPH McLAUGHLIN
LILIBETH TOBILA MACALOLOOY
WILLIAM EDWARD MACK
DOUGLAS EUGENE MALICOTE
WENDY GAY MALICOTE
ELIZABETH LILLIAN MAREK
LOUIS ANTHONY MARENGO
NOEL GEORGE MARTIN
DIANE MARIE MASLOWSKI
JANE SUSAN MELBER
JOHN MERRILL
SUZANNE MARIE MIAZGA
JOSEPH KENNETH MILLER
JEWEL COURTNEY MITCHELL
RICHARD PAUL MONETTI
JANE ANN MORGAN
EVA INGEBORG MORSON
HELGA RACHAEL MOSEY
INGRID ELISABETH MULROY
JOHN MULROY
SEAN KEVIN MULROY
MARY GERALDINE MURPHY
JEAN AITKEN MURRAY
KAREN ELIZABETH NOONAN
DANIEL EMMETT O'CONNOR
MARY DENICE O'NEILL
ANNE LINDSEY OTENASEK
BRYONY ELISE OWEN
GWYNETH YVONNE MARGARET OWEN
LAURA ABIGAIL OWENS
MARTHA OWENS
ROBERT PLACK OWENS
SARAH REBECCA OWENS
ROBERT ITALO PAGNUCCO
CHRISTOS MICHAEL PAPADOPOULOS
PETER RAYMOND PEIRCE
MICHAEL PESCATORE

SARAH SUZANNAH BUCHANAN PHILIPPS
FREDERICK SANDFORD PHILIPPS
JAMES ANDREW CAMPBELL PITT
DAVID PLATT
WALTER LEONARD PORTER
PAMELA LYNN PORTER
WILLIAM PUGH
CRISOSTOMO ESTRELLA QUIGUYAN
RAJESH TARSIS PRISKEL RAMSES
ANMOL RATTAN
GARIMA RATTAN
SUKUJHI RATTAN
ANITA LYNN REEVES
MARK ALAN REIS
JOCELYN REINA
DIANE MARIE RENCEVICZ
LOUISE ANN ROGERS
EDINA ROLLER
JANOS GABOR ROLLER
ZSUZSANA ROLLER
HANNE MARIA ROOT
SAUL MARK ROSEN
ANDREA VICTORIA ROSENTHAL
DANIEL PETER ROSENTHAL
IRJA JOSEPHINE ROYAL
ARNAUD DAVID RUBIN
ELYSE JEANNE SARACENI
SCOTT CHRISTOPHER SAUNDERS
THERESA ELIZABETH JANE SAUNDERS
JOHANNES OTTO SCHAEUBLE
ROBERT THOMAS SCHLAGETER
THOMAS BRITTON SCHULTZ
SALLY ELIZABETH SCOTT
AMY ELIZABETH SHAPIRO
MRIDULA SHASTRI
JOAN SHEANSHANG
IRVING STANLEY SIGAL
MARTIN BERNARD CHRISTOPHER SIMPSON
IRJA SYNNOVE SKABO
CYNTHIA JOAN SMITH
INGRID ANITA SMITH
JAMES ALVIN SMITH
MARY EDNA SMITH
JACK SOMERLI
LYNSEY ANN SMITH

PAUL SOMMERVILLE
ROSALIND HANNAH SOMERVILLE
GERALDINE ANNE STEVENSON
HANNAH LOUISE STEVENSON
JOHN CHARLES STEVENSON
RACHAEL STEVENSON
CHARLOTTE ANN STINNETT
MICHAEL GARY STINNETT
STACEY LEANNE STINNETT
JAMES RALPH STOW
ELLA G. STRATIS
ANTHONY SELWYN SWAN
FLORA MacDONALD MARGARET SWIRE
MARC ALEX TAGER
HIDEKAZU TANAKA
ANDREW ALEXANDER TERAN
ARVA ANTHONY THOMAS
JONATHAN RYAN THOMAS
LAWANDA THOMAS
TOMAS FLORO van TIENHOVEN
MARK LAWRENCE TOBIN
DAVID WILLIAM TRIMMER-SMITH
ALEXIA KATHRYN TSAIRIS
BARRY JOSEPH VALENTINO
ASAAD EIDI VEJDANY
MILUTIN VELIMIROVICH
NICHOLAS ANDREAS VRENIOS
PETER VULCU
RAYMOND RONALD WAGNER
JANINA WAIDO
THOMAS EDWIN WALKER
KESHA WEEDON
JEROME LEE WESTON

MARCH APRIL MAY JUNE 1995

DENVER AIRPORT

Airports are not normally very exciting, but Denver, Colorado, has an airport that conspiracy theorists maintain is more than just a departure point for frequent fliers. They say it's a secret HQ for secret societies.

Denver gained a new airport in 1995, to replace 1920s-vintage Stapleton airport. The new runways were longer, and congestion eased. However, some found the airport's "swastika shape" sinister. Lurid artwork around the airport shows, conspiracy theorists claim, alien languages, Masonic symbols and soldiers in gas masks.

Why were five buildings put up, then buried? Why did aircraft suffer a rash of cracked windshields? The conspiratorial answer was electromagnetic pulses from an underground complex, since Denver supposedly conceals the world's largest underground bunker-refuge against nuclear attack or environmental catastrophe for the elite few who control it. Also underground, so it is said, is a concentration camp for dissidents or anyone who tries to oppose the Illuminati, the New World Order, or even the US government.

Below: Conspiracists allege that cracked aircraft windshields are evidence of unusual goings-on at Denver Airport. Others put them down to weather conditions.

Below: The layout of the runways has led to much speculation. Why so big (the largest airport area in the US)? Were the runways there for modern jets, or to disguise what was underneath the tarmac—or maybe even to signal to outer space?

Above: The swastika symbol has very ancient mystic associations, dating long before it was used by the German Nazis.

Below: The Moon shines above Denver's terminal buildings, but is there a darker secret hidden in deep bunkers underground?

Left: Conspiracy theorists are disturbed by vivid art around the airport. The fibreglass blue mustang with glowing red eyes has been called "the Devil's Horse". Others just don't see it as relaxing airport art.

THE TRUTH?

Denver airport is busier and more functional than the old city airport. The "alien languages" are in fact Navajo words, though Masonic imagery does feature in the art. The cracked windshields were due to weather and bird strikes. The airport does have tunnels, originally planned for trains, but since 2005 used for baggage handling.

MARCH APRIL MAY JUNE **JULY 1937**

AMELIA EARHART

Above: Amelia Earhart (seen here in 1928) was the first woman to fly the Atlantic solo (1932). She was already a celebrity before her 1937 disappearance.

Amelia Earhart was the most famous woman pilot of the 1930s. Her disappearance in 1937 sparked an unsuccessful search of the Pacific, and left in its wake an ongoing mystery.

Enthusiasts for conspiracies suggest that Earhart's disappearance was more than just a flying accident. With navigator Fred Noonan, she took off from California on May 20, 1937. By July 1 they were in New Guinea, having flown 32,000 km (20,000 mi.) in stages. The next day Earhart radioed that the plane was low on fuel. Nothing more was seen or heard of her.

Above: Earhart missed her intended destination, Howland Island, and researchers now think she probably crash-landed on a reef just off Nikumaroro (formerly Gardner Island), seen here. The plane and its radio would have been swept off by the tide. Researchers still hope to find evidence of the castaways.

Howland Island

This map shows Earhart and Noonan's route (actual and unfinished) across the Pacific. It was the most hazardous leg of the trip.

NAME

THE EVIDENCE?

It seems most likely that Earhart and Noonan died as castaways. Air photos taken in 1938 may show footprints, and in 1940 the British discovered human bones on Nikumaroro. Other artifacts found include a mirror, a knife and US-made bottles. DNA evidence could solve the mystery of Earhart's final flight once and for all.

Earhart's disappearance spawned conspiracy ideas. One theory is that she was asked to spy on Japanese naval activity (although the US did not go to war with Japan until 1941), and was shot down and either died or was taken prisoner. Some think she died in a Japanese jail, others that she was freed in 1945 and given a new identity as businesswoman Irene Bolam, until her death in 1982. Or, did she fake her own disappearance, perhaps to elope with Noonan? Her husband, US publisher George Putnam, had her declared legally dead in 1939. The most way-out fantasy is that Amelia Earhart was abducted by aliens—a storyline that found its way into a 1995 *Star Trek: Voyager* episode on TV.

Below: Nikumaroro had no fresh water and little to eat apart from fish, clams and coconut crabs, such as this one. Hungry crabs may have scattered the two fliers' remains.

Below: The plane Earhart and Noonan flew in on their last voyage was a twin-engined Lockheed Electra.

Right: Amelia Earhart was awarded the Distinguished Flying Cross in 1932 for "heroism or extraordinary achievement". She was the first woman to receive this honor.

WHO WERE THEY?

Identity is key in stories of murder and mystery—not just "who did it", but "who were they?" Slipping across the pages of history are mystery men and women, around whom conspiracy theories spin webs of intrigue.

The world knows Shakespeare, or thinks it does, but did a glove-maker's son from Stratford really write all those great plays? Some argue that he didn't. So who was the man behind the famous words? Who, too, was the man in the iron mask, or the disappearing prince? Jack the Ripper is another mystery figure. Millions of words have been written about him, but his identity remains unknown. Anonymous figures often play crucial roles in major dramas—such as the elusive Deep Throat in the Watergate affair. In the cyber-world of Facebook and Twitter, where so many users are keen to tell all about themselves, there are silent movers and shakers. Like sharks beneath the surface, they move through events—but who are they?

MARCH APRIL MAY JUNE

PIGNEROL.

Above: Pignerol, in southern France, where the Man in the Iron Mask was first held prisoner. The governor of Pignerol prison went with the prisoner whenever he moved jails, riding inside a shuttered carriage.

1669

THE MAN IN THE IRON MASK

A famous story by Alexandre Dumas about a masked man held captive for years was based on a real historical mystery.

In 1669 Eustache Dauger was arrested in Dunkirk by soldiers of King Louis XIV of France. He spent the remaining 34 years of his life in prison, his face hidden beneath a mask, his true identity known to only a few. The solitary prisoner was guarded day and night by two musketeers, but was otherwise given comfortable treatment and was fed well.

So who was the man in the mask? (In reality, he wore a velvet hood, not the iron mask of the Dumas novel.) People suspect he was in fact the king's natural father. Louis XIII's marriage to Anne of Austria was childless, and for years the royal couple had lived apart, so it came as a surprise when, in 1638, the queen produced a son. The boy became king in 1643 when Louis XIII died. Rumors spread that the boy's father was not the queen's husband, but a nobleman chosen by Cardinal Richelieu, effective ruler of France, to provide France with the royal heir it needed.

Having done his duty, the bastard father may have been sent abroad, perhaps to North America, far away from the Palace of Versailles and gossip. But should he return...? It seems possible that he did, as "Eustache Dauger," and if he bore a close resemblance to King Louis XIV, tongues would certainly wag. Worse, he might make his paternity known and become an embarrassment to the very regal "Sun King," busy making war across Europe.

Murder was an option, but perhaps King Louis shrank from patricide. Instead, Dauger was confined for the rest of his days, in near-silence and obscurity. When he died in 1703 in the Bastille prison in Paris, he was listed as "Eustache Dauger, valet."

NAME

 EVIDENCE?

A French noblewoman described the man in the mask in a letter to England. She said he had lived and died in his mask, with no-one knowing who he was. The philosopher Voltaire suggested he was the King's illegitimate older brother. Dumas (creator of The Three Musketeers) dreamed up a new plot-line, that the masked man was the King's identical twin. Another theory is that he was an Italian named Girolamo Mattioli, victim of a diplomatic mistake that upset King Louis.

Above: King Louis XIV (1638–1715). He became King of France aged only 4, reigned for 72 years, and liked to be called "the Sun King."

Right: A scene from the 1977 television series *The Man in the Iron Mask*, based on Dumas's classic story. In his version, there are twin brothers: one (the hero) imprisoned behind the mask, the other his brother, King Louis XIV of France. The masked man, Philippe, is the rightful heir to the throne, kept prisoner for wicked political motives, but destined to replace his brother as king.

APRIL MAY JUNE JULY

WHO WAS JACK THE RIPPER?

Below: Jack the Ripper, in a shot from a 1959 British film starring New Zealand-born actor Ewen Solon.

The Whitechapel murders of 1888 spread fear through London's East End. The identity of Jack the Ripper remains unknown.

Five murders in 1888 were almost certainly the Ripper's and two or three others are possibles. All the victims were female, all were prostitutes, almost all the bodies were mutilated, and some had body organs removed. All the killings were done in the same area and over a few months. Was there a conspiracy to cover up the killer's identity? Were there more murders, and why did it take many years for some bits of evidence to reach the public domain?

The Metropolitan Police received taunting letters signed "Jack the Ripper." The first letter, dated September 25, 1888, boasted "my knife is nice and sharp," and one sent on October 16 contained a human kidney. The police were inundated with names of suspects. But were any of them the Ripper?

The police had little to go on other than blood-soaked scenes of crime. Scanty witness evidence suggested the killer was a white male. Could he be a surgeon? A madman? A seaman? A crazed abortionist? Even Prince Albert Victor, Duke of Clarence, and the royal physician Sir William Gull were proposed. Adherents of the royal-killer theory suggested the prince was being blackmailed by one of the victims, and that the government, in league with the Freemasons, moved to silence her, and her friends. Was anti-Semitism involved? A chalked message mentioning "Juwes" was hurriedly erased by police. Sir Melville Macnaghten (who did not join Scotland Yard until after the murders) privately listed his suspects. They included Montague Druitt, a teacher who had lost his job and drowned himself in 1888.

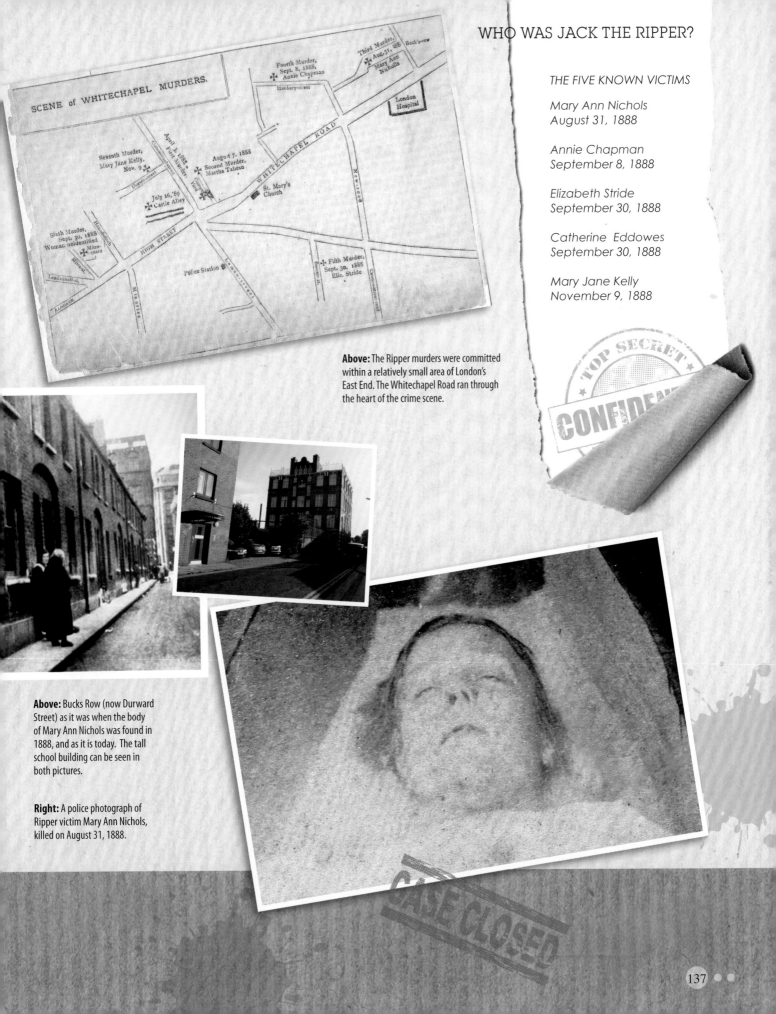

SCENE of WHITECHAPEL MURDERS.

THE FIVE KNOWN VICTIMS

Mary Ann Nichols
August 31, 1888

Annie Chapman
September 8, 1888

Elizabeth Stride
September 30, 1888

Catherine Eddowes
September 30, 1888

Mary Jane Kelly
November 9, 1888

Above: The Ripper murders were committed within a relatively small area of London's East End. The Whitechapel Road ran through the heart of the crime scene.

Above: Bucks Row (now Durward Street) as it was when the body of Mary Ann Nichols was found in 1888, and as it is today. The tall school building can be seen in both pictures.

Right: A police photograph of Ripper victim Mary Ann Nichols, killed on August 31, 1888.

ARCH APRIL MAY JUNE JULY AUGUST–NOVEMBER 1888

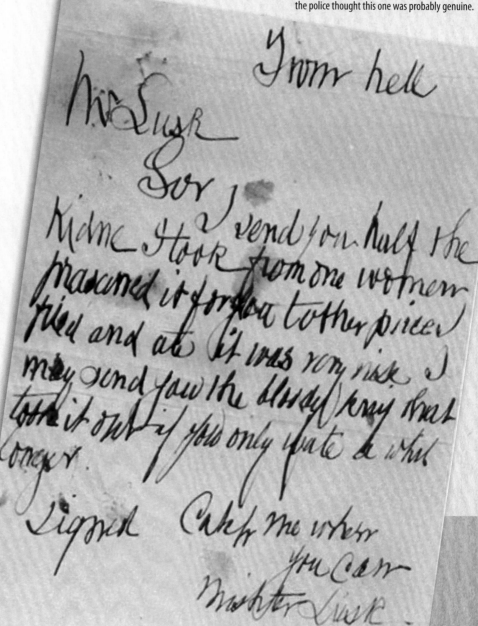

Apart from Druitt, other suspects included artist Walter Sickert, who painted a picture of "Jack the Ripper's Bedroom"; Aaron Kosminski, certified insane in 1891; Nathan Kaminski, who died in an asylum in 1889; and James Maybrick, poisoned by his wife in 1889. Also suggested are Michael Ostrog, Russian con-man; John Pizer or "Leather Apron," a thug who extorted money from prostitutes; and William Bury, hanged in 1889 for murdering his wife. Detective Frederick Abberline suspected George Chapman (aka Severin Klosowski), a Polish hairdresser, hanged in 1903 for murder.

Above: Fashionable men read about the Ripper murders, and wondered, was any one of their class responsible for butchering the Whitechapel prostitutes?

Below: The "From Hell" letter, in which the writer mentions a kidney he has removed from one of his victim and eaten. Although there were numerous hoax letters, the police thought this one was probably genuine.

Above: Prince Albert Victor, Duke of Clarence (1864–92) was a grandson of Queen Victoria. Evidence suggests he was not in London at the time of the Ripper murders.

Above: Walter Sickert (1860–1942), seen here in a 1911 photo, was suggested as the Ripper by crime writer Patricia Cornwell.

some asylum.

No one ever saw the Whitechapel murderer; many homicidal maniacs were suspected, but no shadow of proof could be thrown on any one. I may mention the cases of 3 men, any one of whom would have been more likely than Cutbush to have committed this series of murders:—

(1) A Mr M. J. Druitt, said to be a doctor & of good family, who disappeared at the time of the Miller's Court murder, & whose body (which was said to have been upwards of a month in the water) was found in the Thames on 31st Decr.—or about 7 weeks after that murder. He was sexually insane and from private info I have little doubt but that his own family believed him to have been the murderer.

(2) Kosminski—a Polish Jew—resident in Whitechapel. This man became insane owing to many years indulgence in solitary vices. He had a great hatred of women, specially of the prostitute class, & had strong homicidal tendencies; he was removed to a lunatic asylum about March 1889. There were many circs connected with this man which made him a strong "suspect".

(3) Michael Ostrog, a Russian doctor, and a convict, who was subsequently detained in a lunatic asylum as a homicidal maniac. This man's antecedents were of the worst possible type, and his whereabouts at the time of the murders could never be ascertained.

Above: The Ripper murders featured in this edition of *The Illustrated Police News*, published in London on December 8, 1888.

Left: This is a page from the Macnaghten memorandum of 1894, in response to a newspaper allegation that a man named Thomas Cutbush was the Ripper. Macnaghten listed his main suspects: Druitt, Kosminski and Ostrog.

Above: James Maybrick, a Liverpool cotton merchant, was killed by his wife in 1889. His diary, revealed in 1994, purports to record the Ripper killings, but is not taken very seriously.

MARCH APRIL MAY JUNE   1440

THE REAL BLUEBEARD

Baron Gilles de Rais was a hero of medieval France until his sudden fall, when he was branded a child-killer. But was he set up?

Born in 1404, he fought alongside Joan of Arc to defeat the English; at 16 he'd married a rich heiress; at 24 he was a Marshal of France, patron of the arts and Church, second only to the King. The world was his oyster. Or so it seemed.

Having dissipated his wealth, the Baron turned to alchemy and magic to make gold from cheap metals. His enemies said he'd sold his soul to the Devil. In 1440 Gilles de Rais was accused or sorcery and child-murder, of conspiring to abduct 140 children, draining their blood in satanic rituals to make magic potions. Even in a land used to violent death and torture, such "devilry" caused shock and abhorrence.

Above: Arthur Rackham's illustration from his *Fairy Book* (1913); a little girl is about to open the door to Bluebeard's forbidden chamber. What horrors await?

Right: German actor Hans Albers as Bluebeard in a 1951 film of the story of the rise and fall of Gilles de Rais.

Gilles de Rais was tried in secret. Rather than defend himself, he confessed, admitting his wicked blood-lusts, and was hanged at Nantes. With so little evidence, his friends could not believe his guilt. The witnesses who confessed murders and blood-rituals were probably tortured, and so may Gilles de Rais have been himself. How could he have fallen so far and fast? Was he trapped by conspiring enemies, chief among them the Duke of Brittany? Gilles de Rais made an easy target with his sexual licence and interest in astrology and alchemy; all combined to create an image of a devil-worshipper. Certainly he was no saint, but a child-killer?

The family of Gilles de Rais survived the scandal of his downfall, for by admitting guilt and offering repentance, the Baron salvaged at least some of his fortune, though his castles were taken by Duke John of Brittany. By law, a portion of a repentant sinner's estate remained with his family; had Gilles de Rais fought his case, and lost, they would have lost too.

EVIDENCE?

Joan of Arc, the peasant girl-soldier from Domrémy, led French soldiers against the English who, after Agincourt (1415) threatened to take control of France. At her side at the battle of Orléans (1429) was the young Gilles de Rais. However, the young warlord's bravery, wealth and generosity possibly hid a darker side. After nearly 700 years, it's hard to judge innocence or guilt.

Right: Statue of St Joan of Arc, France's warrior-heroine, at Blois. The peasant girl-soldier trusted the aristocratic Gilles de Rais, who was her gallant lieutenant in battles against the English.

MARCH APRIL MAY JUNE 1793

THE DISAPPEARING PRINCE

Above: A 19th-century engraving of Louis-Charles, the disappearing prince, from a painting made of him in 1792, when he was 7 years old.

Below: Marie-Antoinette says a tearful farewell to her son. The king was guillotined in January 1793 and the queen was kept in solitary confinement until she, too, was executed in October 1793, not knowing her son's fate.

In 1789, revolution threw France into turmoil. Four years later the French king and his queen were dead. So what happened to their son?

Louis XVI, or Louis Bourbon as his republican captors called him, was a victim of the Reign of Terror, the bloodiest period of France's revolution. The guillotine was busy despatching dozens of reviled aristocrats, blamed by radicals for all France's ills under the old regime. King Louis went to the guillotine in 1793, followed a few months later by Marie-Antoinette.

The royal couple had two surviving children (their eldest son died in 1789); a daughter and a son, the Dauphin Louis-Charles, born in 1785. He was 8 years old when his parents were executed, and was given into the care first of a cobbler and then, it's said, of a married couple of gaolers while revolutionary leaders considered his fate. The noble-born revolutionary Barras visited "a boy" in prison in the summer of 1794, and found not the healthy prince, but a child dying of consumption (tuberculosis).

Was this the Dauphin, or an impostor? Years later, the gaoler's wife said she and her husband had smuggled the prince out of prison, substituting a lookalike boy who was dying anyway.

Some officials were sure the dying boy was not the prince. Nevertheless the Dauphin Louis-Charles's death was announced in 1795; whereupon a banker named Petival declared the death certificate to be a forgery. Petival and his family were murdered soon afterward. An odd reference by Barras to "the child you know" being unharmed by this crime suggests he knew Petival had the prince in his care.

Years later, in 1846 and again in 1894, the coffin of the dead prince was opened, and doctors agreed that the bones were those of a teenager aged 15 or 16, not a boy of 10. So what did happen to the Bourbon prince, now in royalist eyes the king of France? When the Bourbon monarchy was restored in 1815, 27 people claimed to be the lost Louis-Charles. One contender, named Karl Wilhelm Naundorff, in 1833, seemed plausible, but Naundorff was shunned by the princess, his "sister," who had survived the Revolution. Naundorff left France fearing arrest or worse and died in Holland, still claiming to be France's rightful king.

Below: The last will and testament of Marie-Antoinette, written while she was a prisoner of the Revolutionary Tribunal.

Inset: Statues of King Louis XVI and Marie-Antoinette, parents of the lost prince of France, in Saint-Denis Cathedral, Paris.

MARCH APRIL MAY JUNE   *1564*

WAS SHAKESPEARE A PEN NAME?

William Shakespeare's plays are the greatest ever staged. True, but who wrote them—the actor from Stratford, or someone else?

Little is known of Shakespeare's life other than the bare facts: a glovemaker's son born in Stratford upon Avon in 1564, he married and had three children, went to London after 1585, and by 1592 was an actor, prolific dramatist (at least 37 plays) and co-founder of the Globe Theater. Rich and successful, he retired to Stratford, where he died in 1616.

"Anti-Stratfordians" claimed that no mere actor, with a grammar school education, could have written plays of such wit, erudition and insight. Francis Bacon was put forward as Shakespeare as early as 1785, followed in the 1920s by Edward Vere, Earl of Oxford, and in the 1950s by William Stanley Earl of Derby. Christopher Marlowe, a playwright who died just as Shakespeare was getting well-known, is another candidate. Bacon, Oxford and Derby are argued to have used pen-names to avoid the social stigma associated with public theater. The arguments against Shakespeare are largely based on the view that he must have lacked the education and breadth of experience, especially of classical literature, history and travel, that a nobleman might have and which is evident in the plays.

In 1796, London's star actor John Kemble presented "a new play by Shakespeare" at the Drury Lane Theater. Titled *Vortigern and Rowena*, the play had in fact just been written by a 17-year-old faker named William Henry Ireland. Kemble suspected Vortigern was a fraud, and mid-performance the tittering audience caught on that the leading actor was hamming up "this solemn mockery." The play closed on its opening night. Undeterred, Ireland continued to pen Shakespeare plays as well as writing under his own name.

Above: Actors in Moscow perform *Hamlet* in a Russian Army production. Shakespeare's appeal is international and his authorship seldom questioned outside academic circles.

EVIDENCE?

NAME

Statesman and scientist Francis Bacon was a brilliant writer; his supporters claim there are "Baconisms" in Shakespeare which could only have been provided by him. Oxford and Stanley were poets, and Derby patron of an actors' company. Marlowe wrote plays of early genius before being murdered in 1793 in a tavern brawl. But was it really Marlowe who died, or a substitute "fall-guy"? If Marlowe was a government agent, perhaps, some suggest, he was spirited away to exile in Italy to carry on writing as Shakespeare.

Above: The modern Globe Theater in London, a reconstruction of the playhouse in which many of Shakespeare's plays were first performed, and in which he was a partner.

Right: William Shakespeare, the boy from a country town in the heart of England who went to London—and made good. Genius can defy explanation.

MARCH APRIL MAY **JUNE 1972**

WATERGATE

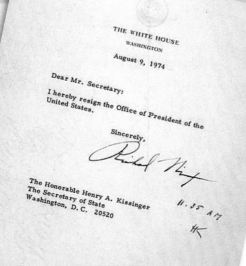

Above: The Watergate office and apartment complex in northwest Washington DC. This insignificant building entered the lexicon of politics and cover-ups. Any "-gate" is now a scandal waiting to be disclosed.

Below On the morning of August, 9, 1974, the day following President Nixon's TV resignation speech, White House Chief of Staff Alexander Haig presented this resignation letter to Nixon to sign.

THE WHITE HOUSE
WASHINGTON

August 9, 1974

Dear Mr. Secretary:

I hereby resign the Office of President of the United States.

Sincerely,

Richard Nixon

The Honorable Henry A. Kissinger
The Secretary of State
Washington, D.C. 20520

11.35 AM

HK

The biggest political scandal in modern US history brought down a president. In the 1970s, "Watergate" became synonymous with "cover up."

In 1972, US election year, the Watergate building in Washington DC was the campaign HQ of the Democratic Party in its fight to deny incumbent President Richard Nixon a second term. A clumsy attempt to break in to Watergate and then cover up the burglary brought seven men, all with White House connections, to justice in January 1973. By then Nixon had been re-elected, and the Watergate break-in was old news—that is, until *Washington Post* reporters Carl Bernstein and Bob Woodward unravelled a tale of conspiracy and cover-up.

Former White House legal aide John Dean admitted a cover-up, and said Nixon knew what had gone on. The president at first refused to make public secret tapes of White House conversations, and when he did, three key conversations were missing. Dogged by a Senate committee and special prosecutors, Nixon eventually released over 1,000 pages of "White House tapes," evidence of a cover-up.

Some 40 people were charged. In 1975 jail terms were handed down to senior White House insiders John Ehrlichman and H. R. Haldeman, and former Attorney-General John Mitchell, for conspiracy, obstruction of justice and perjury.

Nixon faced impeachment by Congress for obstructing justice, abusing presidential powers and withholding evidence. On August 9, 1974, he resigned. He was replaced by Vice President Gerald Ford, who pardoned him for all federal crimes he might have committed.

Below: Four of the original Watergate burglars in police photos: Eugenio Martinez, Virgilio Gonzales (a locksmith), Bernard Baker and Frank Sturgis.

NAME

THE TRUTH?

Information about the cover-up was passed to the Washington Post reporters by an anonymous Washington insider, "Deep Throat." Deep Throat was named in 2005 as former FBI man Mark Felt, though other candidates have also been suggested. Bob Woodward said he met Deep Throat in an underground garage, requesting meetings by putting flower pots with flags on his balcony and receiving meeting-times scribbled on his newspaper.

Above: Nixon's trademark grin on his presidential campaign button. His long political career ended with Watergate.

Right: Richard Nixon at a press conference as the Watergate hearings and press inquiries made him increasingly defensive. Beside him is his son-in-law David Eisenhower.

147

ALL AT SEA

The sea has many secrets in its depths: lost ships, lost treasure, lost souls. Davy Jones' Locker, the last resting place for the drowned, has claimed many victims. In the days of sail, it was common for a ship to leave port and vanish, never to be seen again—its fate unknown.

Sometimes mermaids and sea monsters were blamed for lost ships, but occasionally a ship was found intact, yet without any life aboard, as in the case of the *Mary Celeste*. When *Titanic* left on its maiden voyage in 1912, the mighty liner was said to be "unsinkable", so the world was greatly shocked when news of the ship's fate broke. Today, the story still fascinates, and conspiracy theories about its sinking abound. No area of the ocean is danger-free, but one area of the western Atlantic is said by some to hold the greatest perils. In the Bermuda Triangle, so conspiracists would have us believe, supernatural forces are at work.

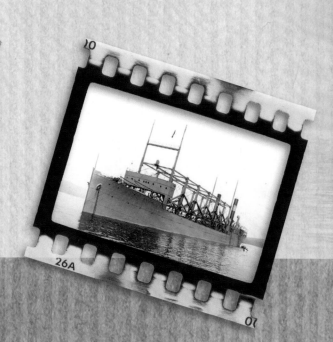

SEPTEMBER OCTOBER

NOVEMBER 1872

GHOST SHIP

The *Mary Celeste* is one of the most mysterious ghost ships in the annals of the sea.

On December 5, 1872, the British ship *Dei Gratia* was about 650 km (400 mi.) east of the Azores in the North Atlantic. Spying a sailing vessel steering erratically, the *Dei Gratia*'s skipper sent a boat to investigate, and found the US-registered brigantine *Mary Celeste*, with not a soul on board.

The *Mary Celeste*, captained by Benjamin Briggs, left New York on November 7, 1872, with nine people on board. The last log-entry was at 8:00 am on November 25, with an unfinished message from ship's mate Albert Richardson to his wife. There was no other clue as to why the ship had been abandoned: reports that the galley fire was still alight, with still-warm cups of tea on the table were not true. An inquiry at Gibraltar concluded the crew might have got drunk (the ship's cargo was alcohol), killed the Captain, his wife and small child, and taken to the ship's boat.

Did the crew mutiny? Did pirates attack the *Mary Celeste*? Or did everyone on board panic, and if so why? There was no sign of a fire or explosion, but something caused the people to abandon ship. Once in the lifeboat, they would have made for the island of Santa Maria, only 10 km (6 mi.) away. However, if a storm had hit suddenly, they would have had little chance in a rough sea on a rocky shore with cliffs.

One possible explanation is that a sailor misread the depth of water in the well of the ship, measured by lowering a sounding rod on a cord down a tube. The *Dei Gratia* sailors noticed the rod lying near its open tube, so "sounding the well" was probably one of the last things the crew did.

After its rescue, the *Mary Celeste* continued trading, until wrecked off Haiti in 1885.

Above: *Mary Celeste*'s skipper Captain Benjamin Briggs. In a letter to his mother before sailing, he said he hoped to have "a pleasant voyage." In their haste, the crew left clothes and even their pipes behind, but Briggs took the ship's papers.

Below: Rum barrels in a ship's hold. The *Mary Celeste*'s crew were unlikely to drink the raw alcohol that constituted their cargo, but fear of an accident may have led to panic.

Below: Painting of the *Amazon*, 1861, renamed in 1869 *Mary Celeste*. After its strange misadventure in 1872, the ship continued trading until wrecked off Haiti in 1885.

A Brig's Officers Believed to Have Been Murdered at Sea.

From the Boston Post. Feb. 24.

It is now believed that the fine brig Mary Celeste, of about 236 tons, commanded by Capt. Benjamin Briggs, of Marion, Mass., was seized by pirates in the latter part of November, and that, after murdering the Captain, his wife, child, and officers, the vessel was abandoned near the Western Islands, where the miscreants are supposed to have landed. The brig left New-York on the 17th of November for Genoa, with a cargo of alcohol, and is said to have had a crew consisting mostly of foreigners. The theory now is, that some of the men probably obtained access to the cargo, and were thus stimulated to the desperate deed.

The Mary Celeste was fallen in with by the British brig Dei Gratia, Capt. Morehouse, who left New-York about the middle of November. The hull of the Celeste was found in good condition, and safely towed into Gibraltar, where she has since remained. The confusion in which many things were found on board, (including ladies' apparel, &c.,) led, with other circumstances, to suspicion of wrong and outrage, which has by no means died out. One of the latest letters from Gibraltar received in Boston says: The Vice-Admiralty Court sat yesterday, and will sit again to-morrow. The cargo of the brig has been claimed, and to-morrow the vessel will be claimed.

The general opinion is that there has been foul play on board, as spots of blood on the blade of a sword, in the cabin, and on the rails, with a sharp cut on the wood, indicate force or violence having been used, but how or by whom is the question. Soon after the vessel was picked up, it was considered possible that a collision might have taken place. Had this been the case, and the brig's officers and crew saved, they would have been landed long ere this. We trust that if any of New-England's shipmasters can give any information or hint of strange boats or seamen landing at any of the islands during the past ninety days, that they will see the importance thereof.

Left: This report on the Mary Celeste inquiry was published in the New York Times on 24 February 1873.

THE TRUTH?

Possibly Mary Celeste was abandoned when Captain Briggs feared a mishap. Did he think his ship was sinking? It's conceivable the crew panicked after misreading the level of water in the hull, concluding the vessel was holed. With his wife and toddler daughter aboard, Captain Briggs may have let his heart rule his head and abandoned ship, only for the ship's boat to be overwhelmed by a rising storm while the Mary Celeste sailed on alone.

APRIL 1912

WHAT SANK TITANIC?

No ship has spawned more words, pictures, facts and fantasy than *Titanic*, sunk after striking an iceberg in April 1912. The tragedy was real, but still surrounded by speculation.

Above: Icebergs are notoriously dangerous because only a small part of the floating iceberg is visible above water, the rest being submerged beneath the surface, a menace to any ship passing too close.

Below: Passengers carried their belongings in trunks and suitcases, each marked with a White Star Line baggage label.

Titanic was the largest ship in the world. In April 1912 it was on its first voyage from Southampton to New York, carrying more than 2,000 people. The North Atlantic that season was particularly dangerous because of floating ice farther south than was usual. *Titanic* received radio warnings of ice, when less than 640 km (400 mi.) from New York. Steaming through the night at speed, it hit an iceberg. Ship's lookouts saw the berg when only 500 m (1,640 ft) away, and alerted the bridge. First Officer Murdoch took evasive action, steering to port and ordering "stop engines" and "full astern." But it was too late to halt 46,000 tons of luxury liner. *Titanic*'s steering was not up to high-speed manoeuvres, and as the ship veered, the iceberg sliced along its starboard (right) side, breaching five of 16 watertight compartments. Designer Thomas Andrews knew his ship could not float for long. He and Captain Smith also knew *Titanic* had insufficient lifeboats. The ship sank in just over two hours, and over 1,500 people died, among them Andrews and Smith.

Controversy surrounded the action of the ship closest to the stricken liner, the *Californian*. It saw Titanic's lights and distress rockets, but did not steam to the rescue until too late. Conspiracy theories came later, the most unlikely that it was not *Titanic* that sank, but its sister ship *Olympic*, the two ships having "switched identities" after *Olympic* collided with a naval vessel and needed repairs.

Robert Ballard found the wreck of *Titanic* in 1985, more than 3,700 m (12,000 ft) down. The ship lies in two pieces, bow and stern sections having broken apart.

CONFIDENTIAL

THE TRUTH?

As so often with Titanic, some choose to believe the unlikely over the probable. Reports at the time were inevitably confused. For example, the ship's musicians went on playing as the ship foundered, but no one is 100 per cent sure what tune was their last, though it was probably the hymn "Nearer my God to thee."

TITANIC
The World's
Largest Liner

WHITE STAR LINE

SOUTHAMPTON ~ NEW YORK
VIA CHERBOURG & QUEENSTOWN

Left: A White Star Line poster advertising the world's largest liner's maiden voyage to America in 1912.

Above: *Titanic* and sister ship *Olympic*. One theory, barely credible, is that the ships were deliberately switched, for insurance and scheduling reasons, and that an accident was supposed to be "staged," but went disastrously wrong. *Olympic* steamed on until scrapped in the 1930s.

DECEMBER JANUARY FEBRUARY **MARCH 1918/1945**

THE BERMUDA TRIANGLE

There is one area of the Atlantic Ocean, the so-called Bermuda Triangle, where a number of ships and planes have vanished over the years, apparently for no good reason. Does the Triangle conceal a dark secret?

The area in question is a sector of ocean between Bermuda, Florida and Puerto Rico. Here some people suggest, ships and planes are lured to disaster. Could they be the victims of unknown natural forces, or darker supernatural ones?

Media interest in the Triangle was sparked in March 1918, when the USS *Cyclops* vanished—probably in a storm—with the loss of 309 crew and passengers. Interest revived in 1945, when five US Navy Avenger aircraft disappeared while on a training flight from Fort Lauderdale in Florida. Radio contact was lost and the five planes were never seen again. It is presumed the pilots got lost, ran out of fuel and ditched in heavy seas, too far from their anticipated position for any hope of rescue to reach them in time.

Such ocean tragedies were all too common before modern navigational aids, such as GPS and rapid-response air-sea rescue. Before the 20th century, and on-board radio, it was not unusual for a vessel to leave port, head out across the ocean on a regular passage, and never be heard of again.

This has not stopped fantastic theories being put forward, however, about the disappearances. These include tales of magnetic anomalies, force-fields, UFO landing sites, and undersea cities, such as Atlantis, with power crystals lying on the seabed causing the catastrophes above!

Above: This map shows the area of the so-called Bermuda Triangle in the Atlantic Ocean.

Below: *Amazing Stories* magazine cover from 1930 pictures a "non-gravitational vortex" in the Atlantic and its effect on ships.

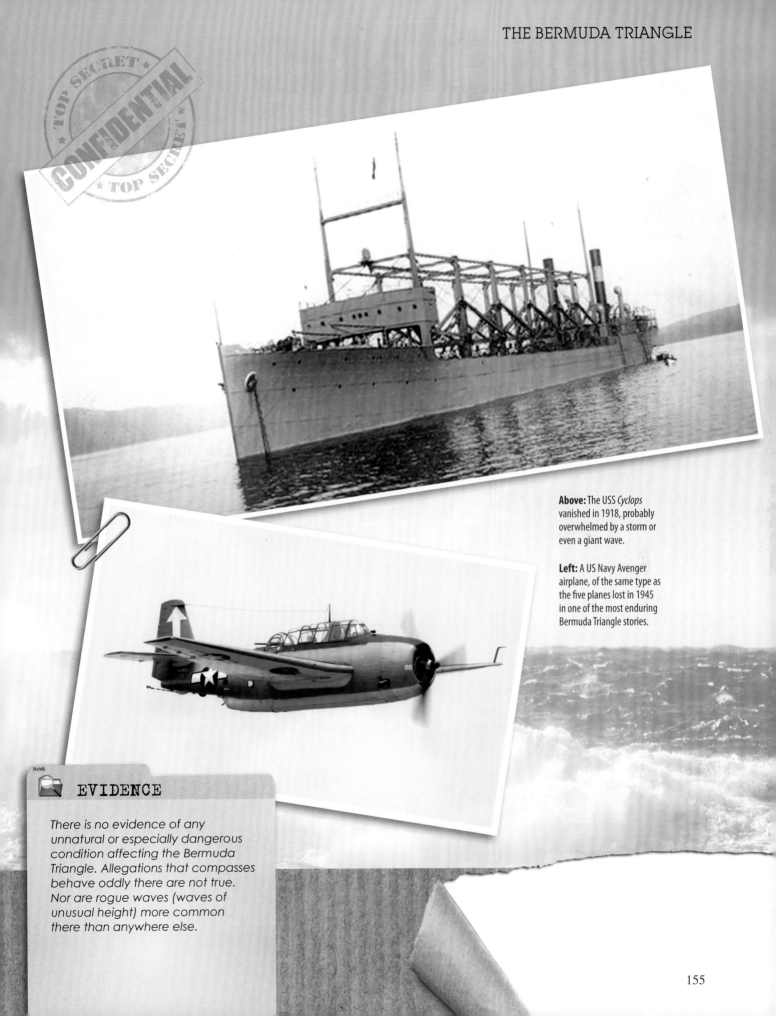

Above: The USS *Cyclops* vanished in 1918, probably overwhelmed by a storm or even a giant wave.

Left: A US Navy Avenger airplane, of the same type as the five planes lost in 1945 in one of the most enduring Bermuda Triangle stories.

NAME

📁 EVIDENCE

There is no evidence of any unnatural or especially dangerous condition affecting the Bermuda Triangle. Allegations that compasses behave oddly there are not true. Nor are rogue waves (waves of unusual height) more common there than anywhere else.

WEIRD AND WONDERFUL

Stranger than fiction are some of the weird and wonderful "facts" that the wilder and more complex conspiracy theories promote. Some are quite harmless, but others at times threaten to spill over into religious, racial, or other forms of persecution and discrimination.

Among the more extreme ideas is the belief that secret societies (or specific groups, such as the Knights Templar) have long been dedicated to covert and subversive operations aimed at world control. Conspiracists maintain that throughout history, secret "string-pullers" have been behind all major events, including wars and revolutions. It follows that world leaders and governments are puppets manipulated by gangsters, religious fanatics, or even aliens. Extraterrestrials, after all, have been interfering in human affairs at least since the time they helped build the Egyptian pyramids, and probably long before!

MARCH APRIL MAY JUNE 1903

SECRET SOCIETIES

Secret societies are claimed to control the world. Most such beliefs are harmless, but myths and lies have on occasions led to persecution and genocide.

The *Protocols of the Elders of Zion* was a faked document outlining a Jewish plan for global domination. First published in Russia in 1903, it was widely translated, with Henry Ford funding 500,000 copies in the United States in the 1920s. The *Protocols* fueled anti-Semitism at a time when Nazi leader Adolf Hitler was brooding his "final solution"— the Holocaust. The *Protocols* were revealed as fake in the 1920s, but are still peddled as authentic.

Freemasons, with their secret rituals and symbols, were suspected of conspiracy from the 1700s. Prominent 18th-century Masons included Benjamin Franklin, Mozart, Voltaire and George Washington. Despite their fraternal and charitable ideals, Masons were accused of plotting the American and French Revolutions, the Jack the Ripper killings, and the downfall of conventional religion. Fears of a "Masonic conspiracy" in the United States gave rise in the 1820s to a political party, the Anti-Masonic Party.

Left: Voltaire, the 18th-century French radical philosopher, was a Freemason. It was the secret society of choice for several notables in Europe and America in the Age of Reason.

Right: An anti-Semitic cartoon from the French *La Libre Parole* (1933). This journal serialized the wildly anti-Jewish libels of the "Protocols of the Elders of Zion," claiming Zionists were plotting world domination.

EVIDENCE?

The Templars have been blamed (or credited) with all kinds of absurd plots, including covering up the "facts" about Jesus Christ's life, the quest for the Holy Grail, and Vatican-centred conspiracies involving mad monks. The truth is that envy of their wealth from banking led to the Templars' downfall, not black magic or sexual misconduct as some suggest.

Wacky and best-selling writers connected both Freemasons and the Knights Templar (also medieval) with secret world government and devil-worship. Charges of Satanism and homosexuality brought down the Templars in the early 1300s. A Christian order of knights to protect pilgrims to Jerusalem, the Templars seemed untouchable, yet their fall was dramatic. Templars were burned at the stake by the French king, but their legacy inspired a host of fantasy-writers.

US conspiracy theorist and academic Carroll Quigley (1910–77) suggested that throughout history "secret societies rule," and that a British imperial secret society founded in 1891 by Cecil Rhodes and Alfred Lord Milner has continued ever since under various names, including the Royal Institute of International Affairs.

The Gemstone File hypothesis suggests Greek billionaire Aristotle Onassis was behind a worldwide conspiracy involving Joseph Kennedy (father of the President) and the Mafia. The Mafia and other groups, such as the Japanese Yakuza, have long been rumored to control governments and corporations, having moved from street crime to the bigger profits of the boardroom.

Above: Jackie Kennedy-Onassis with husband Aristotle Onassis in 1974. Greek shipping magnate Onassis was suspected by some conspiracy theorists to be a "Mr Big" in a covert clique of global power-brokers.

Below: The most infamous secret society, the Mafia, loses another syndicate-boss. Arrested this time was Italian gang-boss Giuseppe Dell'Aquila in 2011, after nine years on the run facing charges of extortion, robbery and money-laundering.

159

MARCH APRIL MAY JUNE 2500 BC

WHO BUILT THE PYRAMIDS?

Above: In 1993, Dr. Zahi Hawass, in charge of Egypt's antiquities, closed the Great Pyramid of King Khufu for a year. Conspiracy theorists suspected the public were shut out so new, "other-worldly" finds could be examined and concealed from the media.

Above: A robot with a camera similar to this fiber-optic "snake" was sent into one of the narrow ventilation shafts deep inside the Great Pyramid. The camera recorded two mysterious doors with metal "handles". What lies behind the inner door is still a mystery.

There are more than 30 pyramids in Egypt. The most famous are the three great pyramids at Ghiza, built about 4,500 years ago as royal tombs. However, conspiracy theories suggest that a veil of secrecy hides the true origin of these mighty stone marvels.

Sceptics doubt official explanations of how the pyramids were built, questioning how massive stones could have been moved and assembled with such geometric precision using manpower alone. Solar and stellar alignment of the pyramids suggests Egyptian engineers were able to calculate the year-length exactly, at 365.25 days. Was such science possible without extraterrestrial help, or guidance from some other more advanced civilization—perhaps the lost world of Atlantis? Ancient Egypt's myth-laden rituals, exotic gods, complex hieroglyphics and monumental architecture fascinate historians, but are also seen by some conspiracists as evidence that our history has been shaped by alien contact. The notion that the Egyptian cosmic-view, with its sky gods and solar boats, was inspired by contact with aliens has spawned a host of theories, most alleging that the academic and political establishment covers up the evidence.

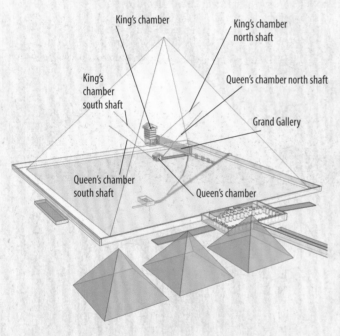

King's chamber

King's chamber north shaft

King's chamber south shaft

Queen's chamber north shaft

Grand Gallery

Queen's chamber south shaft

Queen's chamber

Above: This cutaway plan shows the interior of the Great Pyramid, with its passages, chambers and ventilation shafts. Hieroglyphs were found in a secret chamber in the Queen's chamber south shaft.

NAME

THE TRUTH?

Closing the Great Pyramid led to speculation that Egyptologists were hiding newly found evidence of a lost civilization or alien contact. However, visitors do erode the fabric of ancient monuments and can affect air humidity, so routine closure for cleaning and conservation is not unusual.

Below: The sun at its summer solstice sets precisely between the two biggest pyramids when seen from the Sphinx. Was this alignment achieved with alien help? Could Egyptian fascination with the sun and the cosmos be linked to contact with visitors from other worlds?

Above: The Sphinx is an enigmatic monolith, with grooves (inset) that some people argue were caused by rainwater. If that were the case, the rock could possibly date from a time long before the pyramids were built, when the climate in Egypt was less arid.

Below: The pyramids today attract visitors from all over the world. So awe-inspiring are they that some people find it hard to believe they were built by toiling desert workers alone. Were they perhaps helped by aliens using advanced technology?

161

RELATIVELY RELIGIOUS

Religion has shaped world history and changed lives. Not surprisingly, conspiracy fantasies have drafted startling alternative visions of heaven and earth, and the secret bonds between people and power.

For centuries, politics and government have been inextricably linked with organized religion, of whatever faith. Yet some suggest that there are hidden currents, truths never told (about Jesus for example), secret organizations outside our familiar political-religious structures that really rule the world. This conspiracy tangle assumes a world-view shifting between the supernatural and the pragmatic: where God, the Devil, angels and demons, priests and politicians, philosophers and revolutionaries, all wrestle for power. Conspiracy theories challenge established truth—about the Bible, for instance, about what churches and other religious bodies teach as doctrine, and our notions about who governs us. Is it the people we elect to office, or do they report to secret super-bosses, working to their own agenda?

20-30s AD

THE JESUS CONSPIRACY

The life of Jesus Christ is described in the Bible, but in the absence of much other historical evidence, conspiracy theorists have invented alternative biographies rather different from that taught by Christian churches.

The "Jesus Conspiracy" hypothesis suggests that Jesus had an alternative life-story, a family and a "blood-line", which led to the Merovingian royal dynasty—and beyond. The most wayout theories suggest Jesus was a descendant of Adam and Eve hybrids, created by aliens from Nibiru (aka Planet X). The Turin Shroud is said by some to be proof that Jesus was taken down from the cross alive and survived. His marriage to Mary Magdalene was covered up, some say, as the role of women in the early church was erased by later Christian writers. The Holy Grail cup, at the heart of many Jesus conspiracies, became an icon for historical crusaders—and the fictional Indiana Jones. It was said to have the power to save life, which led to a spate of quests to find the cup.

Above: Mary Magdalene was a follower of Christ, but it is suggested that after a feud between her and Peter, he downplayed Mary's role in the early Church, telling everyone she was a prostitute.

Below: The blood of Christ is central to the Christian mass, or communion. Some say the Holy Grail caught the blood of Jesus as he died. Others suggest the Grail doesn't refer to a cup, but rather to the "sangreal", or "royal blood" of Jesus. It was a coded symbol to protect his bloodline.

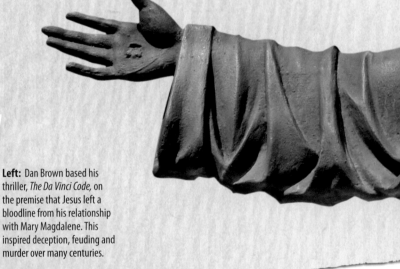

Left: Dan Brown based his thriller, *The Da Vinci Code,* on the premise that Jesus left a bloodline from his relationship with Mary Magdalene. This inspired deception, feuding and murder over many centuries.

Right: Jesus Christ's influence was profound, whether or not you believe he was the son of God. Speculation about Jesus enthrals believers and non-believers alike.

Left: A painting of the Last Supper, from a church in Brussels, Belgium. Some say the Holy Grail was the cup used at this meal.

Below: The New Testament of the Bible is the account of Jesus's life. The four Gospels were written many years after the crucifixion, but scholars believe other accounts were suppressed by the Church.

Below: Glastonbury Tor in England has mystical attractions for people who believe it is where the Holy Grail lies buried. According to legend, the Grail was brought to England by Joseph of Arimathea.

Left: Christians drink wine in remembrance of the Last Supper from a chalice such as this. In the quest for the Holy Grail, seekers sought a chalice (either made of gold or something more humble).

THE TRUTH?

Most scholars find no evidence to support the wilder speculations about Jesus, but conspiracies feed the public appetite for sensational "religion". That Jesus may have loved Mary Magdalene was suggested in the 1200s by a monk, Peter of Vaux de Cernay. The finding in 1945 of a 4th-century Egyptian Coptic text of the "Gospel of Philip", which mentions a "wife", aroused fresh interest.

1776

THE ILLUMINATI

The Illuminati ("the enlightened") were a group of 18th-century intellectuals, but if conspiracy theorists are correct, they became a secret worldwide organization.

Popularized in books such as Dan Brown's *Angels and Demons*, the Illuminati are said to have been behind the French Revolution, Wellington's victory at Waterloo in 1815, and John Kennedy's assassination in 1963. Organized tightly like the Jesuits, it's claimed they even replaced George Washington. Their plan is to institute the New World Order—the world government—and they adopted the Egyptian pyramid and the "all-seeing eye" as symbols. Revolutions and politics were masterminded by the Illuminati, whose members included the composer Mozart, Jewish financiers and a string of world leaders, from Garibaldi and Lenin to modern heads of state. The Illuminati are said to control the economy and media, including the movie industry. Killing anyone who opposes them, be they popes or presidents, is all part of their long-term business plan.

Above: Adam Weishaupt (1748–1830), German rationalist and freemason, founded the Illuminati in 1776, and allegedly took the murdered Washington's place as US President. He told his fellow-Illuminati, "Devote yourselves to the art of deception".

Above: German writers Goethe and Schiller were Illuminati, say conspiracy theorists. Schiller later turned against the order and (according to a 1925 book) was then murdered.

Right: In this re-enactment, French cavalry ride to battle at Waterloo in 1815—one of numerous key events in history supposedly "fixed" by the Illuminati .

NAME

THE TRUTH?

The Illuminati began in Germany in 1776. Its members were influenced by a mix of rationalism, the occult, anti-Catholicism, secrecy and freemasonry. By 1784 the order had 3,000 members across Europe.

Top and above: The pyramid appears on the logo of the US Information Awareness Office, and on the reverse of the US Great Seal, and dollar bill.

Left: Conspiracy theorists point out that the 1789 Declaration of the Rights of Man includes the "Illuminati pyramid-symbol". Was the French Revolution part of the master-plan?

Above: World leaders, such as Queen Elizabeth II, allegedly owe their position to the Illuminati, who eliminate opposition, like assassinated US President Kennedy.

DOOMWATCH

Doomwatchers see plots everywhere, from GM crops to food labels and toothpaste. They also fear that there is a conspiracy to control what we eat, read, think and see, indeed to control our entire lives.

The military, big business and science are in an unholy alliance. Conspiracy theorists see Machiavellian motives in many big business and supra-government activities, including fracking for oil and gas, internet social media, bio-technology, cloning, ocean mining and weather modification. According to some claims, the 2004 Indian Ocean tsunami was the result of dangerous experiments to create earthquake "tidal wave-bombs". Unknown to us, they claim, our lives and thoughts are manipulated by a small cabal, the New World Order or the Illuminati, perhaps linked to such elites as the Bilderberg Group set up in the 1950s. Even vapor trails in the sky could be sinister, for doomwatchers suspect there are a few nasty people hiding out there trying "to fool us and not tell us."

LAST DAYS
LAST CHANCE
ESCAPE HELL
OBEY JESUS

2 COR 6:2
2 TIM 3:1

2 THESS 1:8   LK 12:5

10   26A   10

10   26A   01

MARCH APRIL MAY JUNE

1960s ONWARDS

CHEM TRAILS

Aircraft high above us leave cloudlike white trails across the sky. Could these contrails in fact be chem trails, part of a chemical conspiracy to control an unwitting population?

Airliner jet engines emit hot air into an atmosphere that, at 10,000 m (30,000 ft) or higher, is very cold. The hot gases condense to water and freeze as ice crystals, which stream out as a contrail. As well as water, contrails contain carbon dioxide and other substances, some of which, according to conspiracy theorists, are introduced for covert purposes—to control our weather, to combat global warming, or even to control population growth by reducing fertility or "weeding out" the sick and aged.

Programs such as the High Frequency Active Auroral Research Program (HAARP), it's alleged, "seed" the upper atmosphere with electrically conductive materials, for weapons research or to enhance communications surveillance. Chem trails are linked back to US chemical defoliation tactics in the Vietnam War in the 1960s. They are even alleged to be part of mind-control strategies, perhaps plotted by a covert New World Order cabal (adding chemicals to the air to make people more docile and tractable). In addition, they are altering human evolution, and are part of the worldwide cover-up of Planet X. In certain air conditions, contrails make shadows known as "black rays"—more cause for apprehension and speculation.

Above: Warning symbols for mass destruction, biological, chemical or nuclear, fill people with dread, but what if there are dangers high in the skies?

Above: In the 1960s, the US military used aerial defoliation, spraying chemicals onto forests in Vietnam to deny the enemy cover. This was Operation Ranch Hand (1962–71).

NAME

THE EVIDENCE?

Evidence is slight. Sneak photos of sinister "stuff" hidden in airliners turn out usually to be flight-test equipment, such as water tanks. Scientists do express concern about the effects on the atmosphere of more and more contrails, since the pollution impact of jet particles on the atmosphere is not yet fully understood.

Above: BAE's High Frequency Active Auroral Research Site (HAARP) analyzes the ionosphere to investigate potential communications and surveillance enhancement. Such programs are blamed for everything from bad summers to natural disasters.

Below right: This map shows how fertility rates vary hugely around the world. Some people allege chem trails are linked to population control.

Right: Contrails in a blue sky are a familiar sight, and not just around cities with busy international airports, as here in Frankfurt, Germany.

EXPECTED NUMBER OF CHILDREN
BORN PER WOMAN IN HER
CHILD-BEARING YEARS

7–8
6–7
5–6
4–5
3–4
2–3
1–2
0–1

MARCH APRIL MAY JUNE 1954

NEW WORLD ORDER

Conspiracy theorists claim globalization will bring authoritarian world government. Other groups see the "new order" as apocalypse— a time of judgement.

Some people believe that secretive New World Order leaders are plotting global control. Through wars, our nation states will be abolished, and people will be ruled by propaganda and mind-control. The New World Order would slash the world's population, and bring back a feudal system (lords on top, peasants at the bottom). Genetic manipulation will keep the peasants servile. The New World Order conspiracy is also linked to extremist groups attacking democratic institutions, and to religious ideas about the Second Coming, Antichrist and Armageddon. The end of the world is predicted in various ways (number of popes, days in the Mayan calendar, prophesies like those of Nostradamus…). The politically-oriented New World Order is said to have evolved from the United Nations, the World Health Organization, the G8 rich nations, and the Bilderberg Group (started 1954)—an annual gathering of 100 to 150 influential persons.

Above: A truck-bomb attack on a federal government building in Oklahoma City in 1995 killed 168 and left many injured. It's alleged it was part of a far-right conspiracy to destabilize democratic government. One bomber was executed in 2001, the other given life in jail.

LAST DAYS 2 COR 6:2
2 TIM 3:1
LAST CHANCE
ESCAPE HELL
OBEY JESUS
2 THESS 1:8 LK 12:5

Above: Some religious groups believe that the current world system is doomed in any case, and demonstrate to urge us to prepare for the new order.

Right: Is there somewhere a secret map showing what the world, and its nations, will be like in the New World Order? And if so, who is planning the changes?

Above: The UN flag is a symbol of hope that nations can settle disputes and live in harmony. However, the UN has not proved the world government some hoped it would be after its foundation in the 1940s.

NAME

AT A GLANCE

The Great Seal of the United States carries the Latin tag "novus ordo seclorum" (new order of the ages). The term New World Order described reconstruction after the two world wars, and was used in Hitler's Third Reich. In 1940, H. G. Wells wrote "The New World Order", extolling a collectivist world-state. Post-1945, communists were New World Order architects; today's villains are global capitalists and the state machine.

INDEX

PICTURE CREDITS

1t © ITV/Rex Features, 1c pd, 1b Sh/ © razlomov; 2t Getty Images, 2cl Sh/ © Avella, 2cr © Moviestore Collection/Rex Features, 2b Sh/ © Mario Vazquez-Figueroa; 3t pd, Robert John Welch (1859-1936), official photographer for Harland & Wolff, 3cl Sh/ © Gabriele Maltinti & Sh/ © Twonix Studio, 3cr Sh/ © akva, 3b Sh/ © tarasov, 4t pd, 4b pd; 5t Sh/ © photo video the same object, 5b © Everett Collection/Rex Features; 6 Sh/ © Antonio Abrignani; 7t Sh/ © Kostyantyn Ivanyshen, 7b © ITV/Rex Features; 8bl Walt Cisco, Dallas Morning News, 8br Library of Congress/Alexander Gardner; 8-9 Sh/ © David Kocherhans; 9 (main left) Sh/ © Micha Klootwijk, 9bl Abbie Rowe, National Park Service/John Fitzgerald Kennedy Library, Boston, 9br Abbie Rowe, National Park Service/John Fitzgerald Kennedy Library, Boston; 10t MB PICTURES/Rex Features, 10b pd; 11 main pic Walt Cisco, Dallas Morning News, 11br) © Moviestore Collection/Rex Features; 12t © MEPL/INTERFOTO AGENTUR; 12b pd, Cecil W. Stoughton, White House Press Office (WHPO); 13t pd, Abbie Rowe White House Photographs, 13b pd, White House photographer Cecil Stoughton; 14t © Epic/Mary Evans Picture Library; 14b © KPA/Zuma/Rex Features; 15 (main) Sh/ © Black Russian Studio, 15tr pd, Warren K. Leffler, U.S. News & World Report; 16t Abbie Rowe, National Park Service/John Fitzgerald Kennedy Library, Boston, 16c pd Quarterczar, 16b pd; 17t Sh/ © Balefire, 17c) © Epic / MEPL, 17bl Sh/ © TanjaJovicic; 18t © MEPL/Interfoto Agentur, 18b pd; 19t © ENRIQUE MENESES/Rex Features, 19c © MEPL/Epic, 19b © Roger-Viollet/Rex Features; 20-21 © Mary Evans/Glasshouse Images, 21t Wknight94 talk, 21b U.S. National Archives and Records Administration; 22t PD-RUSEMPIRE, 22b Sergey Nemanov (Photocity); 23 © MEPL; 24bl Sh/ © Andy Lidstone, 24br Sh/ © Olga Popova; 24-25 Sh/ © Adriano Castelli, 25bl Sh/ © Adriano Castelli; 25br Sh/ © Andy Lidstone; 26t pd, 26b © SNAP/Rex Features; 27 (main pic) © Moviestore Collection/Rex Features, 27b © PETER BROOKER/Rex Features; 28t pd, 28b Bettmann/CORBIS; 29t David Shankbone, 29c © Rex Features, 29b Sh/ © Andy Lidstone; 30tl Sh/ © ITS STUDIO, 30bl Sh/ © s_bukley; 30-31 b/g Sh/ © Harijs A.; 31t Sh/ © Andy Lidstone, 31c Sh/ © catwalker, 31br Sh/ © Featureflash; 32bl Sh/ © Georgios Kollidas, 32br Sh/ © Hitdelight; 32-33 Sh/ © Verdateo; 34t Sh/ © Mary Lane, 34b Sodacan{{Inkscape}}; 35 © MEPL; 22t © INTERFOTO / NG Collection / MEPL, 36b Sh/ © c.; 37t © Mary Evans / Peter Higginbotham Collection, 37bl © Geoff Moore/Rex Features, 37br Rasiel Suarez; 38t Sh/ © Zack Frank, 38b Sh/ © Heartland; 39 Getty Images/ Neil Holmes; 40 © MEPL/DOUGLAS MCCARTHY; 41tl Getty Images, 41tr Getty Images, 41b De Agostini/Getty Images; 42 © MEPL/ The National Archives, London. England, 43t © MEPL, 43b © INTERFOTO / Sammlung Rauch / MEPL; 44bl Sh/ © Fer Gregory, 44br NASA; 44-45l Sh/ © razlomov, 44-45r Sh/ © Fer Gregory; 45bl Sh/ © Avella, 45br Sh/ © MWaits; 46t Photograph from the U. S. Department of State in the John F. Kennedy Presidential Library and Museum, Boston., 46b © MEPL; 47t Sh/ © MWaits, 47c © MEPL, 47b Anon; 48t Swedish military photo, 48c pd. United States Air Force., 48b Henrickson (English Wikipedia user) and Foxbat; 49tl © MEPL, 49tc pd, 49tr © MEPL, 49br © MEPL; 50t NASA/ JPL, 50b NASA; 51t © MEPL, 51bl Sh/ © WitR, 51br Sh/ © Avella; 52tl Finlay McWalter, 52cl pd, United States Air Force, 52b Bob Orsillo; 53tr Sh/ © Claudio Divizia, 53 (main) Doc Searls from Santa Barbara, USA, 53bl US Government (the white house) + Colby Gutierrez-Craybill + NASA, 53br pd; 54t NASA; 54-55 Apollo 17 Crew/ M. Constantine (moonpans.com)/NASA, 55tl NASA, 55tr NASA; 56 tl Bubba73, 56tr Wknight94, 56cl NASA/GSFC/Arizona State University, 56cr NARITA Masahiro; 57t Pascalou petit, 57cr NASA, 57br NASA; 58 pd; 59tl Sh/ © welcomia, 59tr NASA, 59bl Amble, 59br NASA; 60bl pd. Public record office, London, 60br Sh/ © Frontpage; 60-61 Sh/ © Carolina K. Smith MD; 61bl Robert, 61br Bundesarchiv, Bild 183-S33882 / CC-BY-SA; 62t Bundesarchiv, Bild 141-1880 / CC-BY-SA, 62b Bundesarchiv, Bild 146-2005-0157 / Unknown / CC-BY-SA; 63t) pd. Lieutenant Louis Klemantaski, Royal Navy photographer, 63b © MEPL/Onslow Auctions Limited; 64t pd. Public record office, London, 64c Sh/ © markrhiggins, 64b Draco2008; 65t Bettman/Corbis, 65b Bettman/Corbis; 66t pd, 66b pd; 66-67 Sh/ © Kevin M. McCarthy; 67tl Sh/ © justasc, 67tr pd, U.S. Navy, 67bl pd, United States Office of War Information, 67bc pd, PD-USGOV-MILITARY-NAVY, 67br Sh/ © catwalker; 68t Bundesarchiv, Bild 183-74237-004 / CC-BY-SA, 68c Bundesarchiv, Bild 183-S33882 / CC-BY-SA, 68b Sh/ © joingate; 69t (left to right) a) Bundesarchiv, Bild 183-S62600 / CC-BY-SA, b) Bob Adams adamsguns.com, c) Bundesarchiv, Bild 183-V04744 / CC-BY-SA, d) Christoph Neubauer, 69br (top) pd, 69br (bottom) pd; 70t Robert, 70c TSGT CEDRIC H. RUDISILL, USAF, 70b pd; 71t Sh/ © Anthony Correia, 71bl Sh/ © Frontpage, 71br pd; 72bl Sh/ © Neftali, 72br Sh/ © Katerina K.; 72-73 Sh/ © RHIMAGE; 73t Sh/ © NinaM, 73bl Sh/ © David Fowler, 73br Sh/ © Featureflash; 74t Sh/ © Ersler Dmitry, 74b Sh/ © photo video the same object; 75t © Daily Mail /Rex Features, 75b © Associated Newspapers /Rex Features; 75 b/g Sh/ © Andy Linden; 76t © Daily Mail /Rex Features, 76b pd. PHC HAROLD WISE; 77t © David Fowler / Shutterstock.com, 77b © Stafford Pemberton/Rex Features; 78t © Paul Fievez / Associated Newspapers /Rex Features; 78br pd.; 79l © kojoku / Shutterstock.com, 79r © Richard Gardner/Rex Features; 80t © BEN JONES/Rex Features, 80b E © vening News /Rex Features; 81t © Featureflash / Shutterstock.com, 81c Sh/ © akva, 81b Sh/ © Patrick Wang; 82tr Sh/ © Neftali, 82bl SOS Fantome, 82bc Erik1980; 82-83 pd; 83tl Abi Skipp, 83tr Sh/ © spirit of america, 83cr Ritzparis - Fabrice Rambert, 83b Sh/ © cinemafestival; 84bl Curecat, 84br Sh/ © Lena Grottling; 84-85 Sh/ © Kesu; 85bl Sh/ © miker, 85br pd, Nasko; 86bl pd, 86br pd, United States federal government; 86-87 Sh/ © fairy_tale, 87cl Curecat, 87cr Sh/ © mikeledray, 87b pd; 88tl Sh/ © molekuul.be, 88b pd, Psychonaught, 88bl pd, 88bc pd, 88br pd; 88-89 pd © Alvaro German Vilela; 89tr pd, Nasko, 89r Sh/ © maradonna 8888; 90bl pd, 90-91 Sh/ © Everett Collection; 91cl Eubulides, 91bl Sh/ © miker, 91tr pd, U.S. federal government, 91r pd, Jack W. Aeby; 92bl Nmnogueira at en.wikipedia, 92br Sh/ © I. Pilon; 92-93 Anrie; 93bl pd, 93br Crypto-Researcher at en.wikipedia; 94 © Chris Barham / Daily Mail /Rex Features; 95t © TREVOR HUMPHRIES/Rex Features, 95b © Nils Jorgensen/Rex Features; 96 Anrie; 97t © Illustrated London News Ltd/MEPL, 97b © NILS JORGENSEN/Rex Features; 98t Sh/ © glenda, 98c Sh/ © Mike Liu, 98b Sh/ Boris15; 99l Sh/ © I. Pilon, 99r pd; 100t Hans Weingartz; 100b Sh/ © Diego Barbieri, 101l Sh/ © Diego Barbieri, 101r Sh/ © Matteo Volpone 102-103 © Daily Mail /Rex Features, 102b © MEPL; 103b Nmnogueira at en.wikipedia; 104t Sh/ © Angie Chauvin, 104b Wilson44691; 105l pd. Fiziker, 105r © Everett Collection/Rex Features; 106t pd. Kahuroa, 106b Sh/ © Eric Isselée; 107l pd, 107b Sh/ © Gorshkov25; 108t © MEPL, 108b Sh/ © astudio; 109l © Illustrated London News Ltd/MEPL, 109r Crypto-Researcher at en.wikipedia, 109 (main pic) Sh/ © Victor Habbick; 110 Arthur Wright (died 1926), 111t SSPL via Getty Images, 111b Paul Glazzard; 112t © National Museum of Photography, Film & Television T / Science & Society Picture Library, 112b SSPL via Getty Images; 113tl SSPL via Getty Images, 113tr SSPL/NMeM/Glenn Hill, 113bl unnamed; 114l © MEPL, 114b InverseHypercube; 115l Sh/ © Tomasz Bidermann, 115r pd.; 116t pd. Library of Congress Prints and Photographs Division. Brady-Handy Photograph Collection., 116b Sh/ © viki2win; 117t pd., 117b © Everett Collection/Rex Features; 118 Sh/ © wavebreakmedia ltd; 119tr Sh/ © James Steidl, 119cl Sh/ © JetKat, 119b Sh/ © Ana Blazic; 120t pd, 120b Hansueli Krapf; 121t Jabberocky, 121b pd; 122bl pd, 122br pd; 122-123 Sh/ © Marcos81; 123bl Sh/ © Jorg Hackemann, 123 br pd; 124tl pd, PD-USGOV-NTSB, 124bl pd; 125tl pd, PD-USGOV-NTSB, 125tr pd, U.S. Government, 125cl pd, 125cr Mgw89, 125b Americasroof; 126t Sh/ © Patrick Poendl, 126b Sh/ © rtguest; 127t Contains Mild Peril, 127c Sh/ © Anatoliy Lukich & Sh/ © achapo, 127b pd, StaraBlazkova; 128b Sh/ © Jorg Hackemann; 128-129 pd; 129tr Sh/ © Jim Vallee, 129bl © Halient/Dreamstime.com, 129br Sh/ © urbanlight; 130tl pd, 130cl pd, Angela K. Kepler, 130b Tentotwo; 130-131 pd; 131tr Brocken Inaglory, 131br pd; 132bl pd, 132br © ITV/Rex Features; 132-133 Sh/ © Lia Koltyrina; 133bl Sh/ © Frontpage, 133br Sh/ © Georgios Kollidas; 134 © MEPL/Epic/Tallandier; 135l Sh/ © abxyz, 135r © ITV/Rex Features; 136 © Everett Collection/Rex Features; 137t The National Archives UK, 137cl Getty Images, 137cr MattHucke, 137b The National Archives UK; 138t The National Archives UK, 138 cl pd, Alexander Bassano, 138bl pd, 138br pd; 139l pd, 139tr Getty Images, 139br pd; 140t © MEPL/ARTHUR RACKHAM, 140-141 © MEPL / SZ Photo / Scherl; 141 Sh/ © CSLD; 142t © INTERFOTO / Sammlung Rauch / Mary Evans, 142b © MEPL; 143l © MEPL, 143r Sh/ © Renata Sedmakova; 144 SID1974 / Shutterstock.com; 145t Sh/ © Lance Bellers, 145b Sh/ © Georgios Kollidas, 145 b/g. Sh/ © Yezepchyk Oleksandr; 146t Sh/ © Frontpage, 146c © Rex Features, 146b © ITV/Rex Features; 147l Sh/ © Pattie Steib, 147r © ITV/Rex Features; 148bl pd, Photograph was taken by the New York Navy Yard, 148br © Zepherwind/Dreamstime.com; 148-149 © AdamEdwards; 149bl pd, Robert John Welch (1859-1936), official photographer for Harland & Wolff, 149br pd; 150t pd., 150b Sh/ © Vinicius Tupinamba; 151 © Zepherwind/Dreamstime.com; 152t © Thinkstock.com/ Hemera, 152b Sh/ © Tish1; 153t pd. Robert John Welch (1859-1936), official photographer for Harland & Wolff, 153b. © Gorgios/Dreamstime.com; 154t Danilo94, 154b © MEPL; 155t pd. Photograph was taken by the New York Navy Yard, 155b Sh/ © LFink; 156bl Sh/ © jorisvo, 156br Sh/ © dreamerve; 156-157 Sh/ © Brian Kinney & Sh/ © Chromatika Multimedia snc; 157 br Sh/ © razlomov; 158l Sh/ © jorisvo, 158r © MEPL/Epic/Tallandier; 159t © MEPL/AGIP/Epic, 159b Sipa Press/Rex Features; 160tl author unknown, 160tr Sh/ © Chris Pole, 160cl R.F.Morgan; 160-161 Sh/ © Gurgen Bakhshetsyan; 161tl Sh/ © Patryk Kosmider, 161tr Sh/ © shin, 161b (foreground) Sh/ © razlomov; 162bl Sh/ © Renata Sedmakova, 162br Sh/ © Jill Battaglia; 162-163 Ekaterina Pokrovsky; 163 r Sh/ © Vinogradov Illya, 163bl Sh/ © Colette3, 163br Sh/ © Atlaspix; 164t Sh/ © Maran Garai, 164bl Sh/ © Jill Battaglia, 164b (inset) Sh/ © Featureflash; 164-165 Sh/ © Alfonso de Tomas; 165tl Sh/ © Renata Sedmakova, 165tc Sh/ © Sorin Popa, 165cl Sh/ © Stephen Chung, 165r Sh/ © Timothy Large; 166tl author unknown, 166bl Sh/ © Kati Neudert, 166br Sh/ © Colette3; 167 (main) pd, 167tr a) pd, PD-USGOV-MILITARY, 167br Sh/ © Portokalis, 167br a) Sh/ © thatsmymop, 167br b) Sh/ © Atlaspix; 168bl Sh/ © Frontpage, 168br pd, USAF; 168-169 Sh/ © Gabriele Maltinti & Sh/ © Twonix Studio; 169bl pd, United States Federal Government, 169br pd, Staff Sergeant Preston Chasteen; 170tl Wikimedia Commons, User:Andux, User:Vardion, and Simon Eugster, 170bl pd, USAF; 171tl pd, Staff Sergeant Preston Chasteen, 171r pd, Sh/ © S.Borisov, 171cb Supaman89; 172tr 169br pd, Staff Sergeant Preston Chasteen, 172bl Sh/ © Frontpage; 172-173 Sh/ © winui; 173tr Sh/ © Dusan Po.